FINAL LECTURES

BOOKS BY KAREN HORNEY

The Neurotic Personality of our Time
New Ways in Psychoanalysis
Self-Analysis
Our Inner Conflicts
Neurosis and Human Growth
Feminine Psychology

Edited by Karen Horney
Are You Considering Psychoanalysis?

BOOKS EDITED BY HAROLD KELMAN, M.D.

(Companion volumes:
Contributions to Karen Horney's Holistic Approach)
Advances in Psychoanalysis
New Perspectives in Psychoanalysis

FINAL
LECTURES

KAREN HORNEY

Edited by

DOUGLAS H. INGRAM, M.D.

W·W·NORTON & COMPANY

New York · London

The text of this book is composed in Walbaum. Composition and manufacturing by the Maple-Vail Book Manufacturing Group. Book design by
Jacques Chazaud.

First Edition

ISBN 0-393-02485-7

W. W. Norton & Company, Inc.
500 Fifth Avenue, New York, N. Y. 10110
W. W. Norton & Company Ltd.
37 Great Russell Street, London WC1B 3NU

1 2 3 4 5 6 7 8 9 0

CONTENTS

ACKNOWLEDGMENTS

Many people have contributed to the preparation of this volume, more than I can hope to thank adequately. Horney's lectures were taped by Marie Jinishian and were kindly donated to the Association for the Advancement of Psychoanalysis by a member and long-time friend, Norman Kelman. It was Dr. Kelman who eventually completed this course that Horney had begun. The esteemed psychoanalyst Marianne Horney Eckardt graciously encouraged the publication of the manuscript and assisted with locating certain obscure references. Still, it was the dogged insistence of Frederick Burnett and his confidence in the worth of this project that persuaded the officers of the association to pursue transcription and publication. I am grateful to its officers, then and now, for their support and trust in this undertaking: Jeffrey Rubin, Henry Paul, Daniel E. Cohen, Leland van den Daele, Leonidas Samouilidas, Joann Gerardi, Kenneth Winarick, James P. O'Hagan, Jeanne Smith, Leonel Urcuyo, and Susan Rudnick. I am especially grateful to Ann-Marie Paley, then president of the association, for her initiative and support of this project. Arnold A. Mitchell provided much assistance and helpful points of view. Edward R. Clemmens contributed his appreciation of Horney's idiom to suggest further enhancements of this work. I

ACKNOWLEDGMENTS

am indebted to Doctors Paley, Mitchell, and Clemmens for proofing the manuscript against the original tapes to ensure veracity. Our editor at W. W. Norton and Company, Hilary Hinzmann, has lent the patience, graciousness, and skill needed to realize this volume.

Others who have helped in often crucial ways are: Herbert M. Rosenthal, Isidore Portnoy, Gerald T. Niles, Morris Isenberg, Harriet Rossen, Philip Bromberg, Joyce Lerner, Barbara Frank, Alisa Chazani, Ronald S. Rauchberg, and Morton B. Cantor.

This edition is dedicated to my wife, Nancy.

—Douglas H. Ingram, M.D.
New York, 1986

INTRODUCTION

When I was a medical intern, a friend encouraged me
to read Karen Horney's *Our Inner Conflicts*. My immediate reaction was amusement and surprise at the
author's surname. Also, I had no special interest in
psychiatry and psychoanalytic theory: for me, psychoanalysis was arcane and bizarre. Yet when I finally took
up the book, I was astounded.

Readers new to the work of Karen Horney are nearly
always struck with self-recognition. Within her pages
they discover their own secret inner strivings, their fears,
doubts, drivenness, and conflicts. Her compelling theory of personality, her capacity to speak directly, and
her courage to dissent from the mainstream views of
psychoanalysis gave vitality to contemporary psychotherapy. Her theory of feminine psychology provided
a necessary corrective to the phallocentric metapsychology that dominated in the 1930s.

Interested primarily in describing neurotic personality, she wrote comparatively little on the technique
of psychoanalytic therapy. Still, at the institute which

9

she founded for training doctors in psychoanalysis, Horney conducted courses of lectures on analytic technique. She was convinced that what the analyst does must proceed from what the analyst understands. The influence of her teachings on generations of psychoanalysts and their patients, and her impact on developments in psychotherapy is ample justification for publishing the edited transcript of her final series of lectures on analytic technique.

Horney's chief success was in helping to free psychoanalysis from a strict instinctivistic and mechanistic conception that prevailed during the first half of this century. The theory she offered as an alternative is one that is primarily interpersonal and cultural: people develop in relation to other people living within a cultural ambience. She held that we transmit to each other a vast panoply of often conflicting values and attitudes—of how things seem, of what is funny or tragic, of what is normal or sick, of what is beautiful or ugly, of what is merely wrong in contrast to what is unspeakable. In health, these become internalized in each of us and enable us to share, more or less, a common comprehension of our world and yet to realize our separate inner potentialities. In neurosis and other forms of psychopathology, this process is subverted.

Horney was one of many psychoanalytic thinkers who assisted the shift in psychoanalysis from the instinctivistic to the interpersonal/cultural. Others included Harry Stack Sullivan, Eric Fromm, and Clara Thompson. Their impact on conventional Freudian thinking encouraged the rise of ego psychology, the evolution of object relations theories, and the development of transcultural psychiatry. Decades later, essential aspects of Horney's focus on understanding, neurotic pride, and the idealized self would be echoed in the self-psychology movement.

In the lectures that follow, you the reader join a course on psychoanalytic technique, officially entitled "Psychoanalytic Therapy" in the *Catalogue of the American Institute for Psychoanalysis*. The catalogue introduces the course briefly: "These lectures do not intend to teach psychoanalytic technique, but rather to present and discuss viewpoints which may help those who so desire to develop their own ways of conducting an analysis." In fact, Horney departed from the defined schedule of lectures, apparently choosing to place first those topics she considered essential. Stricken by cancer, she was unable to complete the course.[1]

Although the class was directed to psychiatrists with at least two years prior training in the practice and theory of psychoanalysis, Horney speaks with a clarity that renders her ideas accessible even to those without advanced training. The lectures retain, beyond the content of her thought, a quality of her personal immediacy. Because her personal impact was so strong, this volume concludes with a reminiscence by Edward R. Clemmens, one of her students in the 1950s.

Above all, we have sought to produce for an enlightened general readership a profound yet accessible insight into an outstanding psychoanalyst's views of analytic technique. Also, to satisfy the needs of the professional psychotherapist without disrupting narrative flow, we have provided an appendix of notes to the lectures.

INTRODUCTION

The course originally began September 15, 1952, and ran on Monday evenings at 8:30. Lectures were an hour to an hour-and-a-half. The class was full, not only with candidates-in-training, but with experienced certified psychoanalysts. In these pages we can join them as they listen to a master analyst explain her working principles.

D. H. I.

FINAL LECTURES

1. The Quality of the Analyst's Attention

We have restricted this course to senior psychoanalysts-in-training at our Institute. That means we are a nice small group which makes for more and better discussion. But, also, it arouses the hope in me that this course of lectures might be more than my presenting something to you, and that we might also look at the course as a kind of research project in which we make efforts toward the goal of improving the principles of psychoanalytic technique.[1] There is no doubt in my mind, at any rate, that there is much reason for discontent with the effectiveness of our therapy. We all have to strive, therefore, for ways to make it—I wouldn't necessarily say quicker, although that is something we also want—but quicker particularly in the sense of being more effective, going more quickly to the core of the trouble and helping more.

I think the course, on the other hand, will offer you more the less you have false expectations. I have tried already to lower expectations in a remark I made in the Institute catalogue, specifically that this course is not meant to teach technique. It was not false modesty on my part because I am convinced we cannot teach psychoanalytic technique, and certainly not in a series of lectures. Contrast a course of lectures, for instance, with analytic supervision in which an analyst-in-training presents his work with a patient to a supervisor at regular and frequent intervals.

In analytic supervision, you can address concrete problems arising in therapy with a specific patient. Let's suppose for example, you have a patient who is always late for the hour and offers plausible excuses with which he is satisfied. Now there you have a concrete issue. In supervision, you and your supervising analyst can explore the particular problems that may be involved. Here, our course cannot deal with such concrete issues.

What we can do is take up the whole question of retarding forces and blockages, of which latenesses and the reluctance to recognize their meaning are but expressions. So what we are doing here is discussing many topics, including the general question of blockages, their meaning, and how to deal with them. That is the difference between what these lectures can offer and what your other work at the Institute provides.

Certainly, when we discuss such principles I will give some examples. I hope you will also help out with some illustrations of your own. That always makes things clearer. Nevertheless, we will by and large stay with the principles. I emphasize this because I have not yet seen a course evaluation from students in which there was not a desperate cry for more clinical illustrations. That's all right. I understand that. I am all for being clear and concrete in illustrating something. But I also think of what may lie behind this cry for clinical illustrations: often it may be the hope that some concrete example might help the student with some current concrete difficulty. While I hope you will learn something by inference from what you pick up in this course, relieving you of concrete difficulties with your patients is not our goal.

Something should be said about personal difficulties. You know, one of the great handicaps in our analytical work is our remaining personal neurotic difficulties. Again, in your supervised analytic work you are able to go into your personal difficulties, reviewing them with the supervising analyst and seeing how they influence the course of analysis. Here, in this course, we will go over such difficulties again, but along general lines. We will take two hours and see what the importance is of the personal equation of the analyst. Again, it is up to you to infer from our general comments conclusions specific to yourself.

Finally, I could make some general remarks that are true for supervision as well as for this course. Technique can only be taught to a limited extent because ultimately technique depends on inner freedom, ingenuity, and finger-tip feelings. These are all important components and belong to the consideration of effective analytic technique. These components can be stimulated, helped a little. But they can't be taught.

Now, I will start with a chapter which is pretty vague and which, for the life of me, I couldn't make more definite. Nevertheless, it is the basis for good work: the quality of the analyst's attention.

There are many things that belong to, or are prerequisites for, doing good analytic work. For instance, the whole question of understanding, of interpreting at the right time and in the right spirit, of having a feeling for dreams, and so on and so forth. But basic even to these prerequisites is a certain kind of attentiveness to the patient. I think there are three categories by which we can describe this quality of attentiveness. They overlap to some extent or, to put it differently, they represent different aspects of the same thing: these three categories of attentiveness are wholeheartedness, comprehensiveness, and productiveness. I will make a few comments about each.[2]

That attention should be wholehearted may seem banal, trite, and self-evident. Yet in the sense that I mean wholehearted attention, I think it is rather difficult to attain. I am referring to the power of concentration on one's work, an absorption in one's work, a being altogether with all one's faculties in the situation—and all concentrated on the work.

This is a faculty for which the Orientals have a much deeper feeling than we do. Also, they have a much better training in it than we. We, as a rule, are not trained in concentrating per se. They must so often concentrate in their exercises, postures, breathing, meditation, and Yoga. But what is self-evident is that the power of concentration is terribly important and can be trained. To illustrate, I want to read you a little example from one book about Zen Buddhism. I will do that in our next lecture. Wholeheartedness of concentration means that all our faculties come into play: conscious reasoning, intuition, feelings, perception, curiosity, liking, sympathy, wanting to help, or whatever.

It is rather easy to see what this wholeheartedness, this focusing on the patient is not: it is not to be distracted. That is already something, something that certainly can be trained. Distractions may arise because of some personal worries. Perhaps if your spouse is sick, or your child, you may find yourself distracted. I would say that if the distraction is so serious that you cannot work, it is better to cancel an analytic hour. But, also, there can be training in self-discipline so that concentration on the work is feasible.

In a deeper sense, not to be distracted also means not to be distracted by personal neurotic factors of your own. There is only one exception, I believe, and that is if neurotic disturbances take the form of irritability, anger, fatigue, or whatever, the ideal thing is to file such disturbances for future reference, to just notice them. If they are acutely disturbing, one may make an attempt at a quick analysis. Of course, one can think only so much in a minute. Nevertheless, if these disturbances are sufficiently severe, an attempt at quick analysis is worth it. After all, you are the instrument with which you work. So you are obliged to keep yourself in good shape and to do so in whatever way you must. Wholeheartedness of attention means being there altogether in the service of the patient, yet with a kind of self-forgetfulness.

This may sound self-contradictory: being there with

all your faculties and yet forgetting yourself. Still, if you think of many situations in which somebody operates with ultimate effectiveness, you will see there is no contradiction. Next time, I shall read you a passage in which Goethe's friend Eckermann describes a headwaiter who did almost impossible feats in waiting on a whole banquet table, feats possible because he was there altogether, with all his faculties concentrated on the one task. And yet, at the same time, there was a forgetting of himself in any personal way.

Another aspect of wholehearted attention is unlimited receptivity, letting everything sink in. Work at those impressions that do sink in, with every way at your disposal. Such impressions may sometimes result from good and sharp thinking, but they may also result from something automatically falling in place. Also, this kind of concentration of which I am speaking involves your feelings and is not just cold detached observation. Unlimited receptivity means being in it with all your feelings.

The feelings I am referring to are those related to your patients, ideally. Again, there seems to be something contradictory with what I said earlier about self-forgetting: self-forget, but be there with all your feelings. Still, you know that one can be emotionally absorbed by a picture, by a piece of music, by something on the stage, by nature—or by whatever—and at the same time almost forget oneself. So, unlimited receptivity includes being there with all of oneself, all one's feelings for the patient or against the patient, liking or disliking, sympathy, disappointment, a hope, a fear, a concern, a wanting to help. The best advice that

I can give is that everything come up, emerge, and at the proper time, be observed.

The second quality of this attention is the comprehensiveness of observation, every possible observation. Now, that point has already been made very clear by Freud in what he described as the free association of the analyst, regarded by him as equivalent to the observing of everything, leaving nothing out—unbiased and unselected.

This kind of observing makes no sense in a way unless we add one factor, namely, DON'T SELECT TOO EARLY. I don't remember whether Freud said that explicitly, but his view simply makes no sense otherwise. You have to select. You are neither a camera nor a sound recorder. Besides, it wouldn't help you any if you were. For instance, when you want to understand what is a trend and what the patient is saying, and you ask yourself, "What is disturbing him?," and, "What is the connection between this-and-that of the previous hour and of this hour?"—in all this you are selecting. You are seeking what is essential.

So, the meaning of letting all sink in can only be DON'T SELECT TOO EARLY. Why? Because often it is just some little inconspicuous thing that may give you a clue. Consider, for example, a session from my work with a woman in which she spoke about her indecision. Suddenly, she announced, "Well, I cancelled my reservation for a boat to Italy." At first, I thought she was somehow being scattered, as she often is, but then I took that in, too. I realized that contained in her sudden announcement was her way of informing me how she postpones everything. This led us to the whole idea of her provisional living without commitment to anything, living only for the time being. She was missing the boat in life.

This is an example you can easily duplicate from your own clinical experience. Such examples might seem, as here, little things that nevertheless show you the way, or, while you are listening very carefully, give you a feeling that your patient is uneasy about something. You don't know if he is holding something back, if he is really uneasy, if he is troubled by something that doesn't quite show itself clearly to him, or whatever it is, you have a feeling about it. Now, this feeling may be very important. If you don't pay attention to that, you, too, may miss the boat in that hour and fail to see what is going on. So, this bears repetition: let everything sink in without selecting or interpreting too early, even including your own feelings. Otherwise, you may miss out on something.

The factors that are most frequently disturbing when we consider comprehensiveness of attention are, to begin with, personal factors. You may just not pay attention to something which, for personal reasons, you may be unaware of. Let's say that a patient is anxious. You may be unaware of just how anxious he is. There may be personal reasons for this or what we may call personal blind spots.

Another factor interfering with the comprehensiveness of the analyst's attention is connected with interpreting too early. For instance, you may listen with preconceived ideas—and please don't believe that only Freudians do it—though they certainly do. I remember from the time I was analyzing within the Freudian model, a time when I didn't feel it necessary to listen as attentively as I do now, we had these quick and easy and too-ready connections such as the association between passive homosexuality and one's having been born to an older woman, between sibling rivalry and competition, and so on and so forth. But it is easy enough to criticize others. Let's better ask ourselves if we are not inclined to do the same thing: do we too quickly ask, "What kind of pride or self-contempt is that?" I mean, we also have our brands of categories. While I hope they are better categories, nevertheless, if you introduce them too early in the course of the attention you bring to the patient, then you don't listen to what is said. You don't let it sink in.[3]

Now, let me say the same thing from a subjective standpoint. By this, I am referring to the analyst's need to know and understand everything quickly. That is a problem that can occur with any theory. If you need to know and understand everything quickly, you may not see anything. I am not just speaking about the need to interpret to the patient. If you must have something in your mind because of your own insecurity or intellectual pride, then you may just need to have a quick labeling, a quick understanding, which means that the comprehensiveness of your listening is bound to suffer. Nevertheless, it is possible, in spite of such obstacles, to let everything sink in. It is something you can learn. This quality of attention is something we learn from our clinical experience and the seminars in which we participate through the years.

But attention to what? After all, since you are not a camera nor a sound recorder there will be some selecting always going on. And it does help, just as when you look through a microscope, to have some idea of what is important and what to look for. Again, I can speak only in very general categories, categories which I only want to mention here because we review most of them again, anyhow.

The first of these categories may be termed "general observations." These are, as you have learned in many courses—I know Harold Kelman, among others, pays great attention to these general observations in his lectures on patient evaluation—of considerable importance.[4] Here again, you know how much one can learn if you simply think of how much more a dancer or a gym teacher gets out of a student's posture or gait than does an untrained person; or how much more a graphologist gets out of handwriting; or how much a voice teacher gets out of a person's speech. I am mentioning this because these things show that skill in making general observations can be trained. This does not mean we have to go into voice training or into particular observations of gait, unless these disciplines especially interest us. But, in general, one's whole power of observation can be trained. Nevertheless, we are particularly interested in changes in facial expressions, in moods, and I need not go into the endless varieties of spoken expressions that may appear and the changes in them that may take place. Still, omitting anything that we may learn from that special basis of observations, namely free association, there is plenty we can learn from observing the general qualities of a person and from just letting our impressions sink in. For example, we want our attention to scan such general qualities as truthfulness, directness, vagueness, diffuseness, courage, moral fiber, and moral integrity. Is the patient contradicting himself without noticing it? Is there much self-indulgence? What is his attitude toward pain, making effort, to anxiety? These general qualities, and I'm sure you can extend the list, are all very important. But what we attend to in our patients, we must also attend to in ourselves, and more.

That is, you need also to pay attention to yourself for you are the tool that pays attention to what's going on. When you get interested, or disinterested, or tired, or irritated, or hopeful, or discouraged—all of these are your own feelings, feelings which may easily show you the way, as we will discuss in great detail later on. At that point, we will be talking about the analyst's personal equation.[5]

Then, too, we need to consider the whole attitude of the analysand toward you. What is his attitude toward your comments? And what about changes in these attitudes? All of this demands our attention.

Comprehensiveness of attention includes consideration of any effort exerted by the patient that comes up at any time. Also, there is the constant attention given to the patient's disturbances and the changes that take place in them, including improvements and impairments. Under what circumstances do they recede? When do they suddenly come into the foreground of the patient's mind? The patient's attitude toward his problems is a very important point about which we will talk in the fourth hour when I speak about the patient's defenses. As you know, the patient's general attitude toward his problems or toward therapy may be in the service of almost endlessly wanting help, needing help, wanting more help, feeling too proud to accept any help, denying problems, embellishing problems, cursing himself for any problems, feeling ashamed, feeling guilty, etc., etc. Does the patient want to perpetuate something or really want to fight through his difficulties? But here there is a whole range of attitudes which are particularly important, and which are among the many factors that we wish to pay attention to. Now, this is all very loosely put because I could just as well include many other factors, such as the attention we pay to dreams. But we will discuss these additional factors in part when we discuss free association.

There is an appalling multitude of factors to which we need to pay attention. Comprehensiveness of attention really does include everything, so much so that it may be frightening. But as you know, there is really nothing to be frightened about. Only the beginner is frightened, and rightly so. You are fortunate to be beyond what we might regard as the sheer beginning stage. Just as with driving, when you begin to drive it is necessary for you to pay attention to many things, including speed, course, traffic laws, pedestrians, traffic lights, battery, fuel—you need to pay attention to all of these. If one enumerates each of these, the task of driving seems very difficult. Yet, in time, driving becomes automatic because you know the different tasks so well. This is no empty encouragement that I am giving you. This kind of development actually does happen. But there is also one other thing: it does happen that the more one understands, the more the observations and impressions fall into line, and the easier it becomes to pay attention to them.

Now then, the third category: the productivity of the analyst's attention.

I would think our attention should be productive. If I describe the analyst's attention first, as whole-hearted, and second, as comprehensive, then it will most likely also be productive. That is to say, it will tax your resources. Again, this is perhaps one of the most difficult things to describe, yet it is of fundamental importance. I have thought of some simile by which I could describe it; a description that I reread recently came to mind as I was preparing this lecture. The naturalist William Henry Hudson was describing the Patagonian plains.[6] Now, these Patagonian plains might seem dull to many people on first reading. There are no mountains, no roaring oceans, no delightful abundance of vegetation. It is all rather monotonous. And yet, these plains were meaningful to this naturalist. They were meaningful to him because there was all of him in it, and he could describe them in a masterly way.

The meaning that these Patagonian plains had for that writer was in their carrying him away. They brought to the foreground of his mind that we need not be cramped, that there is an infinity in our souls, a vastness, whereas so many aspects of growing up, of growing civilized, of growing domesticated are cramped. Even if we are not particularly neurotic, we may find so many things become restrictive or cramped. For him the plains were nature in its raw state, its vastness—nature in its infinity. And because it had an intense meaning for him, he was altogether in it.

Take that example and transfer it to what may happen in an analysis. I am quite sure that two different analysts, or even one-and-the-same analyst in different moods, listening to the productions of the same patient in one hour, may have very different impressions. Perhaps the analyst may think, "Oh, that's pretty dull. He's just repeating himself." You see, if nothing appeals to you, you are not really in the session. I have observed just this, for instance, in supervision when a psychoanalyst-in-training would tell me there really was not much going on. Yet, I would find what the patient was saying and what was going on in the session extremely interesting. So, it is a question of what it means to you, of what you get out of it. If you try to train yourself to be altogether and wholehearted, the session will become more meaningful. And as this happens, then you, in turn, will understand very much more of what is going on.

You may have observed this in yourself: let's say you have listened to the patient for some time and you may not be in the very best shape. You may feel very bored. Yet for some reason you wake up in the middle of the hour—and I use the expression "wake up" in the real sense, if you know what I mean—and suddenly the session is very interesting. It is then that you get productive: something is meaningful. That is one way of describing the strange quality of the productiveness of attention.

There is another way that productivity of attention is a little more accessible to observation. If you are completely with a patient, you can sometimes experience how your resources are tapped. This or that will occur to you. Perhaps it will be something from a play, or the Bible, or something from another patient, or from the same patient at another time, or something from your own experiences. You can catch how your resources are tapped. This is the part of the productiveness of attention which is most easily felt and observed.

There is still a third way by which we can describe productiveness of attention. It is something which I can only describe by analogy. I am referring to the following: If our attention is wholehearted, then things will fall into line. I can only compare it with what may go on at night so that things, by morning, are clear. Perhaps they have crystallized in a dream. There is no doubt that an unblocking of our minds occurs when we are asleep or when not consciously thinking about something. That is all I can say about it. If you are wholehearted and allow your faculties to work, they will set to work and do something: they will be productive.

Productivity of attention, therefore, may be quite automatic. I mean, something comes up, some new clarity, perhaps after the patient leaves the session, or the next morning, a few days later, or perhaps while he is still present in the session. At times, something will set you just thinking. But there is, prototypically, a goings-on which leads toward something falling in line, something being ordered, a connection becoming clear, or at least a pertinent question coming up.

Speaking about productivity and the wholeheartedness of attention, I want to comment on the advisability of taking notes. Usually, when I express my

concerns about notes, people will say, "Yes, but. . . ."
At any rate, from what I have said here, you can see
what I have against taking copious notes. I don't see
how anybody can employ a wholehearted receptivity
and productivity of attention at the same time that he
is anxiously scribbling everything down.[7] It's just beyond
me. I think I made my point clear.

I want to finish here with one question, which is
not very crucial but which, if it is to be raised in this
course at all, should be raised now: "Is analytical therapy a science, or is it an art?" The answer does not
concern me personally. Call it this or that, but what
matters is that analysis produces understanding.
Nevertheless, let us clarify this issue for our own benefit and, also, perhaps for some discussion into which
we may be drawn.

When people say analytical therapy is not scientific, they usually have two notions in mind. It's good
to get these out into the open, to try to know what they
mean. Frequently, they mean by the term "scientific,"
first that the investigator is a so-called objective observer,
that is to say, an observer who excludes as much of
himself as possible, rather more like a camera or a
sound recorder. I want to make two comments about
this. There is no doubt that there are kinds of research
work in which this kind of objectivity is necessary. Let's
say somebody, for whatever reason, is reporting pulse
and breathing rates together with movements of emotions. Consider, for example, the experiments that have
been made by Harold G. Wolff at the Payne Whitney
Clinic here in New York.[8] He has studied how much
stomach juice is produced by a certain emotion or range

of emotions. In observations of this kind, which have very limited value, people are clear about what they are out for, and that is a plus, of course. We can only say, as therapists, that it is not enough to be a cold observer. We can agree to it only in the sense that Zen masters might speak of nonattachment. And what they mean by nonattachment is not altogether easy to understand. The one part that is easy is the following: THERE IS NO PERSONAL AXE TO GRIND. They would say, judge something but don't condemn it. You can like something, but you must not necessarily want to possess it or desire it. I think for us the simplest way, if we don't go very much into the intricacies, is to say that in doing analysis one has no personal axe to grind, no neurotic craving. In that sense, perhaps we would agree with the idea of objectively observing. But that is different from what is usually meant by the expression "objective observer" when used to describe the scientific approach. As a therapist, I don't see how cold objectivity is possible.

I think all I have said today shows what I, at least, think about the concept of scientific objectivity and the therapist's attention. You can be a better therapist, or perhaps you can only be a therapist, if you are with all of yourself in what you do. I don't see, personally, why it is preferable for me to work with a little of myself if I can work with all of myself. And as to accuracy, there are plenty of checks.[9] I am not concerned about that at this point.

Now, my second comment on the question of whether analytical therapy is science or art is this: Often we imagine that something scientific can be learned whereas art is altogether more elusive—you either have the gift or you haven't. I don't believe that this is a tenable distinction. While there are differences in the gifts needed to do successful therapy, and though these gifts are difficult to define, there are also many, many ways of learning technique for doing good therapeutic work. Foremost among these is training ourselves, all of ourselves, to pay attention wholeheartedly. So to make a blanket distinction, that therapists are gifted or not gifted, that techniques can be learned or cannot be learned, doesn't jibe with the facts.[10]

So, that serves as an introduction, so to speak. Next time we will go to the subject of free association.

2. Free Associations and the Use of the Couch

Ladies and gentlemen, last time we talked about the quality of the analyst's attention. I discussed three points: wholeheartedness, comprehensiveness, and productivity. I want to read a passage today from a book on Zen Buddhism in which is quoted a passage by Eckermann from his conversations with Goethe, a passage which describes the quality of wholeheartedness.[1] I think it will summarize all or most of the important points we discussed last time. This is the passage:

> At dinner, at the table d'hôte, I saw many faces, but few were expressive enough to fix my attention. However, the headwaiter interested me highly so that my eyes constantly followed him in all his movements. And indeed he was a remarkable being. The guests who sat at the long table were about

two hundred in number and it seems almost incredible when I say that nearly the whole of the attendance was performed by the headwaiter, since he put on and took off all the dishes while the other waiters only handed them to him and received them from him. During all these proceedings nothing was spilled, no one was inconvenienced, but all went off lightly and nimbly as if by the operation of a spirit. Thus, thousands of plates and dishes flew from his hands upon the table and, again, from his hands to the attendants behind him. Quite absorbed in his vocation, the whole man was nothing but eyes and hands and he merely opened his closed lips for short answers and directions. Then, he not only attended to the table, but to the orders for wine and the like, and so well remembered everything that when the meal was over, he knew everybody's score and took the money.

Well, there you have a description of wholeheartedness and of a person, who, in this particular performance was entirely absorbed in what he was doing— operating with all his faculties while remaining at the same time quite oblivious to himself. This, I think, is a very difficult concept to grasp: at the same time having the highest presence and the highest absence. It is not only difficult to grasp as a concept, but it is difficult to be that way or to act that way. These descriptions are commonplaces of Zen because this is the very essence of Zen. This being with all one's faculties in something is, for them, the essence of living. You see this from the passage I cited by Eckermann. Here was a very ordinary situation and you see how the author's fancy and attention was captivated by the wholeheartedness of the headwaiter. But you know, of course, that such wholeheartedness is a rare attainment. Still, as a goal or an ideal it is good to keep wholeheartedness in mind so we can know how far away from, or how close we are, in approximating it. Sometimes we need to ask ourselves what factors might frustrate wholehearted attention.

I will add one thing. The headwaiter could not have performed in this way without training, skill, and experience. That's one thing on which we must fall back. Without training, such effectiveness is impossible. But then, with training and experience, this degree of absorption in what one is doing becomes possible, at least. There are many passages in Hemingway's *Old Man and the Sea* that describe a similar situation: being all there in the job one is doing.

Now today, we are going to talk about free association. When I prepared these lectures, I had, as usual, failed to examine the Institute catalogue in which this course is described. Quite automatically, I started the course with the topic of the analyst's attention. Then, I looked into the catalogue and discovered that the topic of free association is listed first. I think, however, that there is much to be said for the reverse order and I left it this way because that's the essence I felt last time. Paying attention is for us, as analysts, the primary thing to do. Free association is what the patient is assumed to do, expected to do. How we get its meaning across to the patient is, so to speak, a secondary matter. So take this sequence as an expression of what I feel concerns the analyst first and what concerns him second, of what is essential to his task and what follows.

What do we mean by free association? The term itself has a historical meaning which I don't want to pursue. It has to do, as you know, with the evolution by Freud of his technique. There hasn't yet been found a better name, though this name itself is only historically conditioned. When I thought about it, I asked myself if there were a better short name. I wouldn't know. I could say "unreserved talking," "talking without selection," or "letting yourself go," but these are all descriptions more than names. I think we had better let the historical term stand, provided we know what we mean by it.

The meaning and purpose of free association certainly lies in the capacity of the patient to reveal himself with utter frankness. That is why we tell him to say everything that comes up, and as it comes up. It is different, quite different from any social situation, a fact which Erich Fromm has elaborated in a very intelligent paper, "On the Social Significance of the Analytical Situation."[2] He pointed out how much this unheard-of frankness contradicted social codes and social habits. It is also opposed to, or opposite from, any selection, any figuring out, any disciplined talking such as we find in giving a lecture, talking to your maid, or to a man who is laying your carpet. In all these instances, you speak to the point. Free association is speaking without selection and without holding back.

Another way of describing free association, or another aspect of it, is that it is talking in a state of relaxation. And this is where the term "free" comes in. The term "free" has given rise to many witticisms.[3]

But the term "free" still has a meaning, a good meaning, insofar as it emphasizes that we are referring to associations that are not tied down to any fixed root, to any conventions, or to any immediate purpose. Certainly, the patient may at times really want to get something specific across. That's fine, too. But what we actually mean by free association is the purposelessness of mental productions. There is no immediate purpose other than this: letting things emerge. Free association is an ideal. This means that a patient can free associate only to the extent that he can let go, which in turn is dependent on many factors.

This purposelessness of expression must not be confused with purposelessness of meaning, a simple rambling on. The true purpose, as you know, is in enabling the analyst to get a feeling, an impression, to gain insight into how the patient's mind works.

Let's first recapitulate and be clear about the values of free association. One, naturally, is that free association puts a certain check on withholding by the patient, on his checking or selecting something. You see, there really is the possibility that the more a patient says what comes to mind, the more we really can have a picture of how his mind works, the totality of his mind. Of course, free association can only be approximated. Actually, there are manifold purposes to it with or without the patient's knowing it. He will withhold something, he will stress certain things, he will want to impress, he will be ashamed of something and glide over it. And then there is the struggle of pride versus truth going on most of the time. So, there are manifold purposes. Here, we will see what at its best we can hope to attain through free association.

The second value of free association lies in its helping the patient's concentration. Instead of the patient's rambling on or not knowing quite what to say, he has an obligation or contract to free associate. Because he realizes its desirability, that enables him to concentrate on the job and to really stay with what he is coming for. And this concentration, to the extent he attains it and to the extent to which his spirit is really searching for truth, will help him in becoming productive.

Free association, then, assists frankness of expression by the patient and helps him to concentrate on his part of the work. To put it briefly, free association in its ideal stimulates productivity. Now this goes back to an experience in the annals of every psychoanalytic school. Namely, if a patient talks about himself in a free and unreserved way and in the right spirit, then he will be more productive. The way he will be more productive is expressed differently in different schools.

Freud would stress that memories will emerge. We would agree, but we would emphasize that other things will emerge, as well. A patient may suddenly become aware of a connection that had escaped him, but which he didn't see perhaps even in spite of our having mentioned it so many times. He may become aware of certain feelings in himself, certain drives. This stimulation to becoming more aware, to becoming more productive, is still another value of free association.

Then, of course, free association gives us many clues, some of which we will talk about next time. As you know, we gain a great many clues not only from what the patient says, but from the sequence of what he offers and the quality of their continuity. Also, we gain clues to how a patient goes about the task of freely associating. Finally, free association has the value of placing every patient under similar conditions so that comparisons become possible. There are no two patients who go about it—even patients with equally good conscious work—in a similar way. And that is what we are going to talk about most of the hour today: our attention to how the patient is associating or talking about himself.

When we describe or want to get across to the patient the meaning and importance of free association and want to encourage him to do it as far as possible, we must have several viewpoints in mind.

One is that we must avoid speaking to the patient in technical terms, but instead make the meaning of free association clear to him. And that, I think, we can do only if we ourselves are clear about its meaning and value. I will tell a patient at various times what free association really includes. That is, though you may or will tell every patient at the beginning, "Say everything that comes to mind"—and you really mean everything—you will need to run back to that time and time again. When it comes up, you will also need to go into the difficulties your patient has in freely associating. As you know, every patient experiences quite a lot of such difficulty. It is very important, particularly with patients who are perfectionists, to avoid frightening them. As you know from your own patients in analysis and from those you have seen only in brief consultations, many patients are frightened and discouraged because their analysts have told them they cannot free associate. They feel there is nothing doing, as if free association were something very mysterious. That, of course, must be avoided. What you tell the patient must always make sense and be meaningful.

There are many ways of getting free association across at the beginning of work with a patient. How you choose to go about it does depend altogether on the patient. If you have a patient who is rather uneasy or panicky, you can't talk to him much about free association or what you mean by it, or even mention the term. You will gain a feeling for what the patient can really grasp at this time, and what he cannot grasp. One way, for instance, of introducing the subject is to tell the patient at the beginning that analysis is a cooperative enterprise, that you are bringing into it your intense interest in all that concerns him, your experience, your training, and the fact of your being an outsider. As an outsider with a certain experience and training, you are more likely to have a greater perspective on whatever the patient will tell you, more than the patient himself may have even though he may already know a good deal about himself. On the other hand, the patient has all the raw data. He has lived with himself. And this is what he brings to this cooperative enterprise of psychoanalysis. We have only to help him bring it into awareness, to formulate it, to be clear about it, and so on. But the patient is the one who knows, really. And from this stems the importance of his communicating all that is in his mind without selection.

With patients who are calm enough and understand enough and willing enough, I go to some length to introduce free association at the beginning of analytic work. I say, "You may know a great deal about yourself, but there are difficulties in really saying everything. There are all sorts of temptations that may lead you to avoid saying everything that comes to mind." I mention a few. The patient might fear hurting my feelings. He may feel indiscreet in saying something about people. He may feel something is too trivial, something is unimportant. He may be embarrassed about saying something. But he should please express his reservations rather than use his reservations to hold back. At the same time, I do not detail these difficulties at the beginning, but instead I just say, "Everybody has difficulties with free association. The kind of difficulties you will have, we will do better to pick up on them when they appear—there is no use speculating further about them now."

Besides my advising the patient that he not reserve anything or withhold anything, I stress one further point. The patient needs encouragement to express whatever feelings come up and whenever they come up. Whether his feelings are about what I am saying, or about me in any way, whether his feelings are hopeful or discouraged, annoyed or irritated, cheerful, fatigued, anxious, interested, not interested, whatever, he should try to express what feelings he has. I will return to this subject shortly.

I also wish to make the purpose of the whole thing, of free association, clear to the patient. One can only be related to another person to the extent one really knows what is going on in himself and how his mind really works. And, therefore, to the extent that the patient can be helpful, it is in his interest to speak freely.

Part of this I say at the beginning of my work with a patient, as much as I feel the patient can grasp. This is usually not very much. But then, there is one mistake that is sometimes made (as I know from supervisions), namely, that analysts feel that if they have said something about the importance and the value of free association once or twice, or three times, then it's enough. If I say to an analyst-in-training, "Come, say something to the patient about free association," he is likely to reply, "But I have said that already so often." In a way, one cannot speak about free association to the patient often enough. Of course, the remark must fit the situation. For instance, a patient might tell me much later that in a certain connection he withheld reservations about what I had said, believing them to be wrong, or perhaps believing that I really didn't wish him to be happy, or perhaps because he was annoyed with me for some reason. Acknowledgments of such withholding may come at the end of the same hour or in the next hour. When they arise, I can show the patient how little it serves his interests not to express his thoughts and feelings when they first come up. Again, I use concrete opportunities such as this to stress the value to the patient of saying everything.

Before we go into some difficulties, I want to add some comments about lying on the couch. I have spoken on this already in an earlier course of introductory lectures, but actually the topic belongs here. Again, take my placing it second to free association as reflecting my feelings about its importance. Free association enables complete frankness by the patient. That is really important. That is something to keep a constant eye on. Whether the patient lies on the couch or not is quite secondary: it is subordinate to the entire analytic situation.

What is to be said for the couch? Freud's original contention was that it helped the patient to concentrate. That is still true. Lying on the couch cannot be dismissed as an old-fashioned way of conducting the analysis. It may actually help some patients to concentrate more on what is going on. The difference is only that I don't see it as a condition of analysis, *sine qua non,* but as something I treat flexibly. This is something one needs to try through trial and error, asking if the patient operates better lying on the couch or sitting upright. It is particularly helpful to encourage a patient so he feels free to sit up, lie down, walk around, or whatever he wants—to see in which situation he is most productive and can concentrate most.

Now, many writers have criticized the use of the couch. Lying on the couch produces an indirectness in the relationship with the analyst, they say. This is true. Though, of course, it may be argued that even when the analyst is not confronted, still the analyst is there in the patient's mind. Nevertheless, this objection needs to be taken into consideration. Also, for many patients lying on the couch is a way of making the whole situation less real, less concrete; the patient falls into a half-trance. Also, certain patients, stirred by some new insight, may assume more responsibility when they are sitting upright. Many patients find that lying on the couch is just more difficult because they are afraid. They either need the greater control that comes with the sitting position or they need a feeling of contact with the analyst. While it is good to analyze and understand these situations in time, it is good also to respect them. Whatever is easier, whatever is conducive to greater concentration is all right.

What now about the quality of the patient's associations, the spirit, the "how" of them? I put this ahead, again, because I think it is one of the most important things and because I think it is often neglected. Naturally, those who are beginning are more intent on understanding what the patient is saying, about the content and the continuity. But I think that the more your experience grows, the more you will feel free to concentrate very much also on the "how." One couldn't really say that the "how" is more important than the content. If I should make an oversimplified and therefore not-quite-right remark, I would say if the spirit of the associations, the quality, seems right, then one can concentrate on the content. But actually, simultaneous attention needs to be paid to both.

Now let's survey which factors of the "how" of the patient's associations you would pay attention to.

First of all, attention should be paid to the quality of the patient's interest. By interest, here, I mean his interest in knowing himself, in finding out about himself, or revealing himself. I don't mean his interest in just talking about himself. Most people like to talk about themselves. Let's say the more expansive a person, the more he will want to do that. But this correlation is not restricted to expansive types. It is the quality of the interest that concerns us—is it productive? Is the patient really searching for something? Is he really interested in finding out about himself? Or is he slightly bored? You can observe the quality of interest particularly when you know how eager the patient can be at certain times, whereas at other times he starts with yawning and is just not in it. He just rambles on. I have one patient who does that quite frequently. While she reported on some social situation, this patient said, "My mind is wandering and I don't miss it!!" That is how patients may associate. This is a patient who believes nothing has or should have any meaning. So, naturally, when she was not particularly interested in a problem, she rambled on. She wasn't in it, but just talked about things she supposed I wanted to hear. That kind of thing came up very often in my work with her.

There are many, many ways that patients speak which need to be distinguished from real interest. For instance, there are patients who have a terribly circumstantial way of telling something. Certainly, detail may be very important now and then. But if such detail occurs with a certain regularity, if there is endless circumstantiality, then certainly you have something to pay attention to and wonder about. A certain expansive type may talk very freely and eagerly, but his main motivation may be to show the analyst as well as himself that he actually knows everything and has thought about everything. These are patients who, when you tell them something, will very often respond with, "Oh, yes, I know that already." Or, for others, the motivation behind endless detail may be intellectual curiosity. Intellectual curiosity taking the guise of real interest is something which after a while you will recognize often.

A second factor deserving attention is the capacity of the patient to let himself go, to let things emerge. Naturally, a patient can only do as much as he can. Particularly at the beginning, what emerges will contain very little spontaneity. But in accord with his neurotic needs, he will figure out something. He will come with a program that helps him to control what he is saying. For example, he may be out to solve precisely a certain problem and he may stick to the point. And, after all, that may be something for you to work with for quite a while. Still, his effort to solve a problem is far from letting himself go.

Another peculiarity that we find in considering the spirit of how patients free associate is one which is opposite to this "letting emerge" or "letting go," and might be called "dutifully associating." Patients who dutifully associate have quite a good sense for what the analyst would like to hear, or—it's not necessarily that superficial—for what might be important. So, in a dutiful and somewhat lifeless way, they will go into problems, even in a way that may actually help. Still other patients will immediately try to figure out something. Here again, we have one of the many situations in which we can remind the patient: "Try not to figure things out; try to let things emerge." Reminding the patient of this is effective particularly after a while. At the beginning, there are plenty of things you can understand and be helpful about—even without any particularly free talk by the patient. But then there are problems which neither you nor the patient understand. At such times, it is very difficult to get on with the work unless the patient lets things emerge as they come. These would be the particular times to encourage him to do so.

Another point to consider is the continuity of the patient's associations, the visible continuity. I bring this up here though continuity of associations would seem to belong more under the heading of content than of spirit. But it does also belong to the spirit or the quality of the associational material. Does the patient bring in things that have a certain connection? Certainly, you may always feel a reservation if you don't see a connection. True, it may be that you just don't see it. But I would also put some stock in whether the connection is fairly visible, or does it look as if the patient was jumpy and scattered or even had a complete flight of ideas? Of course, you can easily discern extreme examples of connectedness or disjointedness in the sequence of associations. Nevertheless, there are many transitions where you are not able to easily discern the degree of continuity. Ask yourself if you overlooked something and just didn't make a connection, or was there really a jumpiness on the part of the patient?

Again, discontinuity is not our entire concern. On the contrary, the highly controlled patient will stick with an iron determination to a certain problem—should Johnny go to this-or-that school and why this question is so upsetting—and he may stay with this issue for the whole hour. The controlled patient may come with that program and stick to it. You have continuity, but there are so many other things that are missing.

Another factor worth addressing under the heading of the quality of free associations could be described as lucidity, concreteness, or, perhaps, pertinence. In my experience, there are few patients who give you a really lucid description of what has happened. Why that is so difficult is something amazing. I am aware that we all distort things. But even with distortions, unavoidable distortions as they are so wonderfully presented in the movie *Rashomon* and as they are demonstrated in certain psychological experiments—even with these unavoidable distortions, few patients will describe what happened with their child or husband in a clear report of who-said-this and who-said-that. You rarely see the thing clearly before you. When it does happen, I am inclined to regard it as a very positive sign of great integrity.[4]

Or what if, on the other hand, the patient speaks about something with vagueness and diffuseness? Don't seek the reason, yet. Only go so far as to ask to what you should pay attention. What's important there? Or how evasive is he, not only in what he is telling you, but in his responses to whatever you may comment on? Or how easily does he talk about himself or how much about others, about the problems of others? Or is he inclined to make a quick and often imperceptible transition from speaking about himself to speaking about something more general? I don't know how often I have fallen for that! That is very deceptive. For example, it looks and may partly be that many patients really want to be clear about the factors constituting democracy, or in determining what independence really is, or in knowing what true freedom is. Of course, we are always glad to impart our knowledge, and that is all right up to a certain point. Still, it's important to pay attention to this lest it be a kind of unconscious maneuver by the patient to divert things from very personal, subjective, and concrete issues to something more general and more abstract.

Another point to pay attention to is this: No matter how good and productive associations are, is there a fairly free flow in what the patient is saying, or is he under pressure of some kind? Is he working and talking against odds? That may be very apparent even to the patient. Speaking under pressure may show as difficulty in starting the session. He may make long pauses. He may be anxious. He may feel uneasy. Nevertheless, while these signs are easy enough to observe, there are more subtle disturbances which require a great deal of sensitivity from us. Even when the patient tells us about what has happened or about what is going on in him, we want to sense any uneasiness, uneasiness that may be due to many, many factors—perhaps to something that he is holding back or something he is anxious about, and so on.

It is not only these haltings and silences that we are concerned about. There are many other manifestations of the patient's being under pressure. But I use this general term advisedly—the patient's being "under pressure." In fact, such pressures may show in a manner opposite from haltings and silences as in the patient who is impatient, or hurrying, or wanting to get something solved, or talking very quickly about something, and who may or may not be irritable about it. He feels rushed. Again, that may be very important. You may discover that something like this is occurring when you pay sufficient attention to how inner pressure shows. What to do about it we will discuss later.

Last but not least are the patient's feelings. Pay attention to what he feels and when he feels it. Now, with many patients feelings may prove very meager, particularly at the beginning of therapy when you may only be able to get a very barren, clinical report of what has happened: "I saw my relatives then-and-then and at the end I was tired, and while I was there I felt irritated." There is nothing about why such feelings occurred, just what went on. Also, when the patient brings in his own reactions, he may be talking "about" what he had felt. In the example I just cited, the patient noticed he was quite dissatisfied and irritable but he is merely talking "about" something. It is very important to encourage the patient to express what he feels when he feels it. There is no doubt that the patient will come forth and express more of his feelings when you ask him. If he feels you are really interested, he will respond to your interest. He must feel you are interested when he is sobbing, or crying, or anxious, or irritable, or distrustful, or discouraged, or embarrassed, or when he feels relieved. And the more you encourage him and show interest in these feelings when they occur, the more he will respond by bringing something out.

This is, by the way, a remark of more general validity—it does not only concern feelings. The patient will talk more about things as he senses you are listening and really interested in these problems.

All of these points are important, also, with regard to changes that occur as the patient becomes interested or more interested, or when he is fatigued, or when he is systematic, or when he can be spontaneous. We want to consider changes up and down, as well as changes in the whole process of the analysis. All of what I have said is important with regard to changes in what the patient spontaneously offers, as well as in his changing reactions to your interpretations or to your comments. All these factors are important, also, in regard to changes occurring in what the patient tells you about his feelings or his responses to you and to the analytical relationship.

There is a last point to be mentioned here: the question of the patient's productivity. As a result of the patient's being ready to let the analytical process work and his possessing the right spirit, we need to pay attention to how productive he is. Or, to put it from a somewhat different angle, we need to consider how active he can be on his own behalf. Patients show the greatest variations in productivity. Some people can at times be very active in bringing forth material, in seeing connections, and in actually doing some of the analysis on their own. Sometimes, they even tend to want to do it all. But, at any rate, they are active. Patients may also be quite active between hours in their concern about problems. But we generally get only a scanty report about what they have done at those times. Again, still other patients are quite passive. They are willing to toll you what is on their mind, as much as they can, but their attitude is "There you have it. Let's see what you can make of it." You may need to pay attention to this passivity and work with it a long time.

The patient with whom I had the greatest difficulty on this score was one who, when I spoke about cooperation in analysis, about what he brought to our work, and about how he had to reveal himself, said that first of all he didn't like cooperation. But also, he asked, why didn't we have x-rays! He didn't want to be even that active. This is an extreme example. The subtle expressions of attitudes of this kind are important. Consider dreams: some patients who are interested in a dream will bring material to it in their own way, will be very interested in what comes out of the dream, and what the dream may mean. Others will tell a dream and not be interested in it at all. Instead, they just dutifully tell the dream. They will make no attempt at active interpretation. They will wait for the analyst to see to it. They will say, "You are the expert," and give various other ways of rationalizing this kind of passive attitude.

Now, I have not gone into reasons for all of this, but rather I prefer to make a certain survey of what to pay attention to with regard to the quality of the patient's associations. I am sure that one cannot pay enough of just this attention. We will return to this particularly when we talk about blockages because many of the patient's difficulties can be recognized. And you can find access to them if you pay this kind of attention. Attention to the quality of associations will often reveal inner obstacles more than will attention to the content of what the patient is saying.

Next time, the title of the lecture is "Specific Psychoanalytic Means of Understanding the Patient." Admittedly, I make a somewhat arbitrary distinction when I discuss paying attention to the "how" of the associations here and to the content of associations in the next lecture. But we will in the end, I think, find it a useful distinction.

3. Specific Psychoanalytic Means of Understanding the Patient

---

Last time, we started to talk about understanding the patient. In addition to certain general helps we have from our common sense, from the theory with which we are working, and from our experience, there are certain helps specific to psychoanalytic therapy.

One of these is paying attention to what I call repetitive patterns of associations. I don't want to go into detail about this because we have already discussed it elsewhere.[1] A second help, which I prefer to discuss now, comes from our attention to sequence, context, movement, and process. Here, as a matter of fact, is one of the values of free association: you can draw certain conclusions from how associations generally follow each other from one session to the next. Conclusions may be drawn also from the sequence of associations in the same hour.

For instance, I am thinking about an hour yesterday in which a patient talked partly about what he called his hatred of communism and partly about the deadness of his emotions. What came out of it? What's the connection, I wondered, between these two themes that kept recurring together, interwoven? Finally, I found a clue by making a connection with certain things that occurred in the previous hour. In that hour, as in this, "communist" meant for him a power that was inhuman, cold, ruthless, and with complete disregard for the individual. It was something out to smash the individual, a power that was inaccessible to reason. I said to him, "There must be something of this power, as you characterized it—cold, inaccessible to reason—in yourself." Nothing much came from that comment, but the two themes kept recurring until, at the end, he started talking about a certain dilemma he had that same evening. He was supposed to go to a meeting in the service of a cause in which he was really interested. On the other hand, he would like to stay home alone and think about his own problems. "So," he started to say to himself and to me, "after all, when one is really interested in a cause, one should do something for it even if it is inconvenient at a certain point." All right, that sounded fine. But at the same time, a voice in him said, "You are a traitor if you don't go, even if it kills you, even if you have to beat yourself down. YOU HAVE TO GO." This was just at the end of the hour and I could only say, "There we have it, getting at your 'communist'. . . ."

In this episode, there was a suppression, a relentless suppression of all this man's individual feelings.

Whether he liked something or didn't like it—it didn't matter. He didn't count. So there was a connection between these two recurring associations. This is one of many examples which we are easily able to multiply.

Naturally, something else about the sequence of associations that you all have learned and tried to apply as well as you can is the sequence that occurs between consecutive hours. I almost hesitate to repeat this because I suppose you have heard it so often: but you do need a vision, a memory, of what really went on in the previous hour in order to know where you stand. I will give you an example from work with another patient because it also throws a light on certain other points that I want to take up presently.

In this example, the whole context of the patient's interest was in his incapacity to say "no," an incapacity he wanted to be rid of. We had worked on this issue from several angles. In this one hour, he came up with a fear of what a certain friend would do to him if he would not be compliant, that this friend might undermine the patient's job entirely. He had told me a great deal about this friend and I knew that such an action by the friend was totally unlikely. I knew, however, that this friend did have a sharp and facile tongue. My thinking about that helped me to understand what injury my patient really feared, namely, criticism. I brought it up. I asked whether his fear of injury, this harm through perfidious action—whether it was not all standing for his terrific fear of criticism. Well, with some further prodding, the pervasiveness, intensity, and astonishing amount of feeling arising from his fear of criticism did come out. The next hour, he showed anxiety. It soon appeared that what I almost had expected and, in fact, had indicated in the previous hour, was coming to pass. Here was a person, my patient, who was very proud of his independence. He had a real feeling for independence. But this independence was not factual because he was quite dependent on several people and also to a marked extent on the opinions of others. This helped us to understand his exaggerated fantasy of what his friend might do.

So here was an obstacle: anxiety. My patient and I talked about this clash between his cherishing independence, about the illusory part of it, and about his factual dependence on others, created by his enormous, incredible sensitivity to criticism—not only to past criticism but to possible criticism.

The next hour continued along these lines with his realizing how inhibited this fear of criticism made him, that he always had to be on his best behavior, correct, lest he incur criticism. Following that (and I don't know whether it was the same or the next hour), we explored how this fear of criticism would actually prohibit spontaneity. With that, a new anxiety arose in my patient because he valued spontaneity more than anything else. Yet he saw he could not possibly let go as long as his fear of criticism, and whatever motivated it, was also operating. As long as fear of criticism was operating, spontaneity was positively dangerous.

Here you have a condensed presentation of some consecutive hours. Note, too, that in consistently working at a problem a patient indicates his real interest in the problem, and nothing, in the end, will block him. He runs up against anxieties, sees this implication and that implication, but he presses on with the work.

Partly, you can help this along by attending to the trend the patient is really working at. By your own alertness to it, you can keep the patient to the point.

Another important aspect in our consideration of the sequence of associations is attentiveness to things disappearing, or seeming to disappear. In this instance, the difficulty in saying "no," which troubled the patient greatly, had seemingly disappeared. Actually, I had gone on to his fear of criticism which had an obvious connection with his difficulty in saying "no." This was not a real disappearance, but a seeming disappearance. Sometimes, a patient approaches some problem on his own or maybe in response to an interpretation of yours, but he cannot tackle it yet. So the problem disappears, or seems to disappear. We should be aware when that happens.

Now, what is still more difficult is to be aware and to understand the sequence of associations over longer periods. I will give as an example part of a patient's report on his own efforts at self-analysis, but which makes the point very well.

During the summer this patient had the following experience: He had become aware that all his life he had put up with too much, that he had allowed others to ride all over him. He had only been aware of this before in a spotty way. But now it arose as a real emotional experience with tremendous rage at all kinds of people from whom, as he felt it, he had taken too much. He was fully aware that it was good to let these emotions come to whatever extent they existed. He had a full experience of this almost violent resentment. This was followed, this great emotional experience, by a profound feeling of liberation. He felt free, happy, and spontaneous, as he had not felt in a long, long time.

He knew he had hit upon something very important. He tried to go on with it, but couldn't. It was just a closed book. Much as he tried this or that, much as he tried to find associations to his resentment, there was nothing doing. It seemed futile and he gave up. Something else, however, did appear in the following weeks, and that was an increasing awareness of his being more irritable than he thought he had been previously. When he returned to analysis after some months, he reported the following experience, unaware of its connection with the old one: he had visited some friends and three times in one day had pretty much the same experience. The first occurred in conversation about a common friend. He said that he didn't think much of that person. The friends he visited said that that person had quite some qualities and really performed in a remarkable way in such-and-such situation. The patient asked, "Well, what do you really think are his good qualities?" At the same time, however, he was aware that he felt it awfully nice of him to ask such a question.

Second episode: The children of the friends he was visiting came home after having been away and played in the guest room where our patient was sleeping. Already a little irritable, he asked his host, "Would you mind telling the children to leave the room? I want to get some rest." He felt that it really shouldn't have been necessary to ask this and that it was awfully polite of him to do so.

Third episode: They met a couple and my patient had no positive response to these people. He felt he didn't like them. But knowing that his hosts were quite fond of these people, he said, "They really looked very nice." Again, he felt this was very kind and awfully polite of him.

Now, after this repeated itself three times, he caught what was going on. But he made self-deprecating comments, such as, there must be something in him which was awfully arrogant and demanding, demanding of immediate attention, demanding there should be no contradictions, if he said something, that was how it should be, and so forth and so on. We drove home the connection to that very profound experience earlier that summer in which he felt such violent resentment toward those from whom he felt he had taken too much. Apparently, something had come to awareness about his own self-effacing trends. He then felt a great many things about his putting up with so much and his being very nice about it. As it turned out, his responses in those three episodes actually had nothing to do with the circumstances. Rather, he realized how much his own arrogant demands that he not be imposed upon had led him to vastly overestimate how polite he was in each episode.

It is important for you to draw the connection whereby you can get a full picture. Then, retrospectively, you can get an understanding of why your patient didn't get on with himself at an earlier point. In the example I just gave, the patient just needed to catch on, theoretically speaking, to his expansive drives. He did so very timidly and hesitatingly, in recognizing more and more how much his irritability was a frustration of these expansive drives, which included his arrogant demands.

The next thing we discussed, my patient and I, was the intensity of his feeling of liberation after letting loose his rage. Together with what came up in this piece of analysis, we could now understand his feeling so liberated. We could describe it in various ways. We could see the tremendous strain under which this person lived in having to be "so nice," and from which he was feeling liberated. You could also see the tremendous hatred he must have toward others as a result of his own self-effacing trends. At any rate, retrospectively, this liberation became clear. I think this example shows the value of keeping an eye open and remaining aware of the big sweep, of asking what is going on there and why does it not go on at another instance?

To conclude our discussion of associations, I wish to emphasize the importance of their sequence and movement. We cannot be too aware of these questions: Why just now? Why is a memory coming up just in this context? Why is a dream occurring to the patient at this point? Why is this thing dreamt at a certain point? Why does a patient feel angry or disappointed at one moment and not another? Why is he ready to quit something, let's say, when there doesn't seem quite a sufficient reason for him to do so? And so we have these questions with which you are all familiar and which in time we learn to ask of ourselves quite automatically.

Now I come to understanding emotions, our fourth topic. You all know that in dreams the safest clue to the understanding of a dream is in the feelings of the patient as he has them in the dream, whatever they are. Something very similar is true for the occurrence of all emotions. And, again, no matter what emotion it is—whether the patient is crying, sobbing, interested, disinterested, fatigued, listless, liberated, disappointed, discouraged, hopeless—whatever feelings he has are always an important clue. Take, for instance, what I said about this intense feeling of liberation in the example earlier. I am sure we still have to understand more about it than I indicated, but there is something of an intensity in the experience—the rage preceding it as well as the liberation following it could not be greater. The intensity of the emotion shows the way to something very important for the patient. Equally so, whenever anxiety occurs, as in this condensed example I gave you about the fear of criticism in which anxiety appeared twice, there is something to take cognizance of and to be understood. In both these instances, anxiety meant this patient was running up against a conflict.

If one really wanted to get everything out of attention to emotion, one would need to consider the context of emotion here as everywhere: when does the emotion appear? In this example, one would have to understand the meaning of the feeling of liberation, of the anxiety, and of the intensity of the emotion, all of which point to something very important being at stake. That the context of emotion is valuable stems from our observation of all the contradictions and discrepancies shown by the patient.

When I speak of contradictions, I naturally speak of contradictory statements actually spoken by the patient. That happens frequently enough, sometimes even in one hour, sometimes—if you pay sufficient attention—over a longer stretch. For instance, something that occurs frequently is that one-in-the-same patient at one time speaks about his being self-sacrificing. At another time, he tells us about his vindictiveness. Or, a patient will tell you at one time that she cannot carry a grudge, yet sometime later she will tell you about her retaliatory fantasies. Here, two things are important: namely, how much is the patient disturbed by these contradictions? Does he notice them in fact or does he fail to acknowledge them even if you point them out? Also, the patient's rationalizations will often make it a little more difficult to pin down these contradictions. A patient, for instance, who in part presented herself as self-sacrificing and, on the other hand, told me about how vindictive she was, would always feel very justified when she was vindictive; that was the thing to do, for her. Otherwise, she wasn't vindictive. Well, of course, it is important to pay attention to that, too. I mean, under what conditions does a person become vindictive? But the point here is not to be distracted from recognizing the fact of contradiction, whatever its circumstances.

Another contradiction which is always important to observe, analysis or no analysis, is the discrepancy between what a person says and what he does. You will all have many observations of this sort of thing. For instance, a patient professes to have a very vivid and profound interest in analysis, but comes late all the time, forgets an hour, doesn't really change, often isn't *in* the hour. You will wonder about that. Again, it is not enough simply to take cognizance of it, but you have to ask yourself, "What may be behind this?" Very likely it is a conflict of some importance. Or, a patient who professes never to hurt anybody, never to hurt anybody willfully, at any rate, actually seems to do so quite often. Again, here is a kind of discrepancy which you would like to understand. Or, from the example I mentioned before, a person emphasizes his independence very much, but in actual life gets dependent on this or that person as well as being more generally dependent on others' opinions.

Another kind of discrepancy or contradiction is between the surface attitude of a person and his quite contradictory impulses. I remember, for instance, a patient who was very gentle, quite on the resigned side, and noticeably self-effacing. When he started the analysis, there were fantasies and impulses toward me of violence of a remarkably crude kind. Of course, one way for thinking about this discrepancy would be to ask what interests him about starting an analysis. What does it mean? Does it humiliate him to accept help? Does the analysis, as such, frighten or threaten something important? That's one legitimate way for thinking about it. But even before we come to this point, we must be attentive, not so much with the reason for the discrepancy or to the approach we take technically, but more simply to the recognition of something not jibing: the crude, often obscene violence in this patient is discrepant with his pervasive gentleness.

Something similar applies to dreams. A person very smooth in his way of living may seem quite shallow. There may be no observable depth of troubles. But then, in his dreams, there is despair, there is murder, there is wild destructiveness of all kinds. Again, certainly you want to understand the dreams, but the discrepancy there, the discrepancy *per se*, is something to pay attention to and something you want to understand.

Finally, is there a contradiction or a discrepancy between a person's attitude to himself and his attitude to others? For instance, one patient believed nobody should criticize her. A very great anger, an indignation, would arise in her if that should happen. On the other hand, she felt entitled to criticize most freely and abundantly everybody around her. This generally masqueraded as analysis. She typically told others, "The trouble with you is . . . ," or she would tell me about intense degrees of vindictiveness she found in others. Again, another time, she told a friend of hers, who I felt was only moderately vindictive, "One shouldn't be vindictive. After all, understand and forgive!" While she, herself, would get back at everybody or feel an intense indignation if anybody asked her a personal question, she would start "analyzing" someone after knowing him two minutes, or three at best. While she readily felt that others pried into her affairs, she was oblivious to just how much she pried into theirs.

All of these inconsistencies, contradictions, and discrepancies are very important and deserve our attention and quite some thought. They help us in discovering and in understanding something about the discrepancy between the actual self and the idealized image of a person.[2]

So far, I have talked mostly of how we use our faculty of reasoning to see possibilities. For instance, perhaps a person has pervasive claims. You start thinking, "What could make these claims so necessary to the patient?" Or, you start thinking upon seeing a certain attitude of a patient in certain situations. Let's say a patient declares to you that nothing has any meaning and nothing should have any meaning. You may think, "What may that mean in terms of his attitude toward the analysis?" You may think about what a certain dream symbol means. What does it really mean, these two subjects coming in context, coming up in a close sequence? Or, you raise the question, "Why is something coming up at this point?" With each of these questions, there is plenty of good, hard thinking to do. But there is another faculty which may be just as important as our reason, and that is intuition.

What role does intuition play in understanding? I think there are four ways in which it shows. Before discussing them, I wish to say that by intuition I mean a direct understanding that does not entail a process of figuring out or reasoning out—an immediacy of understanding, in other words.

The first of those ways by which intuition helps our understanding could be described as an automatic applying of viewpoints like the ones presented here. It's just like a driver who is experienced. He will not always think, "There is a curve in the road so I mustn't pass this car." He will just not do it. Similarly here. Many of these viewpoints and others will operate in you as you gain experience and you will apply them quite automatically. Here is an instance (this is not a very good example, but it happened in the last few days) where such an automatic grasp operated: A patient came in with a dream in which he had a vague feeling that there was a ghost somewhere. He thought to look over his shoulder, but was somewhat afraid. Finally, he did look and there was a ghost. The ghost was so very real that he got scared and woke up. My automatic response was that he was facing something about himself, something terrifying. Of course, it was no great feat for me to suddenly intuit this. But my point is that I was not thinking. Thinking alone might have led me to the same result very quickly. But there was no thinking. My response was automatic. Maybe you can bring better examples. No better one occurred to me just now.

Another way in which intuitive faculties operate are in what one might call intuitive associations that show the way. I'll give two examples. One was of a patient who told me about the death of a friend. While she talked about it, probably in a way which impressed me as not quite genuine, I thought of the end of Ibsen's *Wild Duck* where the little girl has shot herself. Her father starts to enact the fantasies he lived in. Someone said in the play, "In nine months, little Hedwig will be nothing more to him than a theme for recitation."[3] That was apparently what I sensed. But I did not sense it as clearly as my association showed it to me, and which was right. The other example is a patient

66

who tended toward acting out things which he became clear about. He was in a process of wanting to liberate himself from certain dependencies, particularly from that on his wife. In this process he acted out by hurting her in this way or that way. And while I listened to him, a mystery story occurred to me which I had read years ago. The title was "Malice Aforethought," and it concerned a country doctor who was quite self-effacing toward a very domineering wife. He tried this way and that way to liberate himself but could not do it in any way, partly because it was really difficult, but partly because of his own tendency to comply, to knuckle under, to give in, to avoid asserting himself (which he could not do). Finally, at some provocation, he poisoned her. All this I told the patient. And he said it reminded him of a fantasy in which he was in the basement and he saw a hammer lying around and he thought he might hit his wife on the head with it. That certainly showed that my association was right. But that was not the really important point. What really mattered was the question it brought to my mind: Is not what is going on here an acting out of a certain violence because this particular patient was not really yet ready to tackle his self-effacing trends, which would have been the thing to do? These intuitive associations are quite helpful and I am sure you can bring in examples of it.

A third expression of such intuitive understanding is our own emotional responses to something, feelings we may have without understanding why. We may at times feel very sympathetic to a patient, and at other times, though he complains and is seemingly miserable, we may feel rather irritable. Of course, it may have something to do with us—we must always examine that. But often such responses, even when they offer no immediate understanding, prove very telling as things go on. Unless I have reason to assume "It's me," I take these emotional responses as quite important. When I feel free to laugh about something or when I'm worried about something—these feelings help. To reiterate, there is often an intuitive understanding of what is going on, of what the patient can stand or cannot stand, or what he needs at that time without my needing to reason it out.

And finally, in what is perhaps the most important way intuitive faculties operate—one that I mentioned already when I spoke about the productive quality of whole-hearted listening—things do fall into place. There is so much to be understood, really, about a patient. When I think about all these viewpoints which we have to apply all at the same time and consider that each patient is different, each complicated, I don't quite believe we could do it all by dint of reasoning. But if we have an open mind and if our creative faculties do operate, many things do fall into place, ordering themselves.

Both reason and intuition are important. Trusting our intuition alone, we might easily get lost. Working with our intellect alone would be impossible, or, if possible at all, would be quite barren after a while. These two faculties have to operate together.

Before I finish these comments about understanding, I want still to mention another kind of help, which, astonishingly enough, so many analysts neglect—

namely, the help to be elicited from the patient. After all, we talk about analysis as a cooperative enterprise in which we enlist the patient in order for the procedure to be fruitful and constructive. But as a cooperative enterprise it follows that when you don't understand something, why not sometimes ask the patient? I don't think I have given any supervision to an analyst-in-training in which this has not come up. A colleague might say, "I don't understand this—why does the patient say this and then this?" Or, a supervisee doesn't understand why a patient dwells on some particular point. Very often, under these circumstances, I will say, "Why not ask the patient?" Present the problem to the patient. Sometimes he can even answer it. And your saying, "I don't understand, could you say what occurs to you?" will stimulate his own associations. So, through a real cooperative effort, we will get further understanding.

4. Difficulties and Defenses

We talked the last two evenings about understanding the patient. Now, understanding the patient would not be so difficult if we could count on an equally great willingness by the patient to understand himself, to appreciate himself, to accept himself, and to go through all the steps that are necessary to accomplish self-understanding. Our understanding the patient would not be so difficult if the patient were to have this attitude, come hell or high water: "I want to know who I am, how I am, what I am doing, and how I can change whatever is not desirable." As you know, we cannot count on such an attitude in the patient, or if it is present, it will be there only at times. This was one of Freud's very fundamental discoveries, realizing how in psychoanalysis we are working against odds. He called this resistance. Nowadays, we are hesitant for various reasons to use this same term. I am not yet quite sure whether there is something wrong with the term, but what for us constitutes an obstacle or a blockage or a resistance is something quite different from what Freud meant. Therefore, it might be better to use a different term.

For example, Freud's use of the term *resistance* puts too much onus on the patient. Freud took the term resistance from physics and from the fact that conducted electric currents inevitably meet with resistance. So the original term itself doesn't say anything as far as analytical practice is concerned, and the concept itself doesn't say whether the difficulty that arises starts with the analyst or with the patient.

Naturally, Freud was at first interested mostly in the patient and in what seemed the patient's unwillingness to accept certain interpretations, or the patient's unwillingness or incapacity to change. However, while it is true that Freud was interested in this phenomenon in the patient, he also recognized very early that there could be difficulties on the part of the analyst. Even if you mostly follow Freudian concepts, you could go to great lengths, as has been done already, by recognizing more and more the difficulties contributed to analytical therapy by the analyst. I'll just remind you of Frieda Fromm-Reichmann, who, at least to some extent, grounds her work on Freud's theories, and who certainly has made great strides in recognizing the difficulties contributed by the analyst.[1]

Another fundamental objection to the concept of resistance is that the concept is too little differentiated, too generalized an idea. One could hardly object or criticize if one sees the phenomenon precisely as Freud

71

saw it. One will be unable to see certain broader implications and be unable to recognize the limitations of
Freud's conception. One will only see the phenomenon of resistance as Freud described it.

Now why am I bringing this up here? It is not so
much for the sake of going into polemics with Freud.[2]
You have opportunities for that in other courses. I bring
it up because there is some lack of clarity in this earlier
concept and we may gain new clarity if we start with
our own concept. The generalization that Freud made,
and to which I object, was that everything could be
called resistance which retards the analysis. But that
would include or concern all neurotic difficulties. Freud,
on the basis of his concept, has said that a particularly
strict superego or an intense narcissistic attitude may
constitute such a resistance. Please translate that into
our concepts. We would say things such as a patient's
compliance, a patient's tendency towards self-accusa-
tion, his externalizations—all of these are retarding
factors. They present difficulties in therapy. Thinking
along these lines, you would then have to say that
blockages are the patient's own defenses, which he puts
up against analytical therapy and which are pretty much
identical with his obstructive forces. I want not so much
to question this concept, but to arrive at a clearer definition of it.

In this regard, today's lecture is different from those
before and probably different, also, from those to follow, because in other lectures I talk about usages,
opinions, and factors that I feel reasonably sure about
and that have become established, more or less. Here,
in speaking about retarding factors, I venture into

something new, groping for clarification.

I think that the first step towards what I am presenting today, I made long ago in my book *Self-Analysis*. I suggested that resistance, or however you wish to call it, was the patient's tendency to maintain the status quo. Later on, I enlarged the definition to include not only the patient's wish to maintain the status quo, but his wish to improve the functioning of his neurosis. That is, he wishes to maintain his neurosis but without the difficulties and disturbances arising from it. The differences in these concepts of resistance no longer seem important to us. Earlier, when I regarded resistance as the need to maintain the status quo, I made the distinction between the neurosis itself and the need to defend it. This distinction was not really clearly defined and, recently, I had to make sure of what I had written. I reread the chapter "The Road of Psychoanalytic Therapy" in my last book, *Neurosis and Human Growth*. From the point of view that I am presenting today, what I wrote in that chapter seems not at all clear.

Partly, when we say that blockages are the odds against which we are working, we mean that they stem from the obstructive forces in the patient. Partly, that is quite all right. We use the term obstructive forces to mean forces blocking the patient's growth. That is, they are not altogether *destructive* in nature. If, for instance, a patient is driven to be helpful—compulsively helpful—that may, at times, be quite useful for other people and, indirectly, for himself. Or, an attitude of mastery, the feeling that there is nothing he couldn't do, may at times give him a good impetus to tackle real difficulties and, in that sense, also may have definite usefulness. It remains to be stated, however, that the term "obstructive forces" has this quite specific frame of reference, namely, obstructing the patient's growth. In a way, in therapy, the same vantage point obtains because we would like to help the patient towards his own growth. Whatever is obstructing his growth and his development in real life, will also obstruct his own and our attempts to help him towards growth in therapy. His mastery, his planning, his control, his squelching of self-doubts, arbitrary rightness—these are disturbing his growth in general and would also disturb psychoanalytic therapy.

So far, we are saying that blockages are particular ways in which obstructive forces show in the psychoanalytic process. They will show there in particular ways just as they show in particular ways at school, or in a job, or towards work, or in a marriage.

However, if we put it that way, then to speak of blockages or resistance is rather redundant because then it would mean that the odds against which we are working are really those same neurotic difficulties for which the patient is coming for treatment. Or, we might say that psychoanalytic therapy is difficult because the patient comes with all his neurotic difficulties—and we, as analysts, have to contend with these. This may be clearer if we compare it with organic illness.

Think of a fracture or any other organic illness. The surgeon has to deal with certain difficulties in the fracture. Is it a compound or a simple fracture? How easily can it be straightened out? Are there infections? And so on and so forth. But actually, the surgeon would—

as physicians always have (though that is made more explicit these days)—distinguish between the difficulties in the illness, let's say, the fracture or the tuberculosis or the cancer, on the one hand, and on the other, the patient's attitude towards the fracture, the patient's attitude towards getting well, the patient's attitude towards the doctor. I would like to raise the question: Is there something equivalent in psychoanalytic therapy? We cannot expect it to be as neat and clear as in the case of organic illness, but is a similar distinction possible?

We all tend to make a naive distinction between the disturbances with which the patient comes—let's say, his anxieties, his rigidities, his prides, his vulnerabilities, on the one hand, and on the other, his withholding things, his lack of incentive, his not cooperating, his always forgetting things, his disregarding interpretations. We make this distinction emotionally, so to speak, because when we start to think about it, we find such a distinction makes no sense at all: the patient's withholding something is just as much an expression of his neurotic structure and difficulties as is his anxiety. Or, his refusal to test what the analyst addresses to him—his assumption of rightness, for example—is as much a part of his neurosis as is, let's say, his psychosomatic disorders. Yet, we have a somewhat different attitude towards each of these two categories of difficulties. I said it makes no sense if we think about it. But our attitude or feeling that these are truly distinct categories is there if we examine ourselves carefully.

Let me approach it from a different angle. What is

our dream of the ideal patient? That would be a patient who we grant comes with all his difficulties. We cannot but grant that. That is to say, he comes with his pride, with his vulnerabilities. These factors which operate in the patient are also directed towards ourselves within the analytic process. When we call his attention to a particular pride or vulnerability, to all his ways for saving face, the ideal patient would be eager to learn about it. He would say, "You are right. Let's examine the darn thing!!" Surely, this hypothetical, ideal patient withholds things, consciously or unconsciously, for whatever reasons, but if we note the withholding and show him "Here you have been withholding something and this is not profitable for the whole process," and if we show him quite exactly the ways in which something is damaging, he would say, "By golly, you are right!" And he would be, again, very eager to examine this and, eventually, to change. Or, let's say we show him his unproductive way of living or he becomes more and more aware on his own of his unproductive way of living, that he is not really using his resources, not being creative, not being happy, or whatever, then he would be eager to see what accounts for it, eager to take a stand, and to find a more productive orientation. Although I say this is our dream of the ideal patient, it's not altogether fantastic. Such things may happen. Those of you with more experience may have seen patients like this at times.

I will give one example here that may lead us a step further. This patient has impressed me quite a lot and I have cited her work in analysis on various occasions before. She is a very effective head of a social agency:

a good organizer, a hard worker, very devoted to her work, and very much convinced of the value of labor unions. At one point, the social workers organized themselves into a union and she was all for it. It was a deeply ingrained conviction of hers that this was a good step. But, as is natural in such a development and particularly with a union, there was now a certain tension. While there was good cooperation with her workers before, now began a time of transition in which her workers were rather militant. She was the boss and they were fighting for their rights even if it was, perhaps, not so very necessary to fight. She was terribly upset about it. She came to ask my advice, anxious, and quite dissolved in tears. We talked about it. There were two neurotic factors involved of which I mentioned only one, namely, her need for affection—and I could add, certain claims related to that need: she had been such a good boss (which she was). I mean, she had always been attentive to the workers, their feelings and their needs. Once she understood these tensions as transitional, her neurotic need for affection and her claims for appreciation by subordinates subsided. Well, this discussion took only two hours, yet it had a dramatic effect in helping her to drop this excessive need for affection and in getting her to recognize the situation as it was. Very soon, she was once again on very good terms with her workers.

Now why could she do that? There were pretty strong neurotic factors involved: her need for affection was very great and so were certain claims. But there were other values at stake which to her were very much more important. There was her conviction about unions, for one. Even more important, she had a profound devotion to her work, and if her need for affection and its associated claims interfered with the effectiveness of her work by creating tensions all around, they had to be dropped—and they were. This might look as if there were only constructive forces acting and that she could call on them. That is not quite so. There was also, as I recognized later, another factor that made this quick change possible, and that was her deep belief, "It's just me, just personal factors." These factors—which we earlier recognized as her neurotic need for affection and her claim that she be appreciated—she felt shouldn't interfere with the work to which she was so devoted. At any rate, here were values involved that had very much more meaning to her than this neurotic need and claim. If her devotion to work—and to her analytic work—had not prevailed over neurosis, one could very well have assumed that she would have gone on the defensive and said, "Well, after all, I always have been a good boss. They could really trust me. They could really have confidence in me," and so on. Yet, she didn't say this.

So in this instance, it is not the neurotic difficulty per se that makes for therapeutic difficulty. Our question is, does the patient go on the defensive for these attitudes that come up for discussion? This patient explores rather than defends. In other words, it is a matter of the patient's attitude towards his own neurotic needs, claims, and so forth. The same applies to any other situation. The patient comes with his pride and his vulnerabilities, or his face-saving devices or his avoidances. These are the difficulties with which he comes. And they do make for difficulties in treatment. But it seems profitable to distinguish these difficulties from the defenses he puts up to protect these difficulties. That is to say, what counts is, does he go on the defensive for his pride, for example? Or, is he willing to examine things?

This is why I have called this lecture "Difficulties and Defenses." The meaning is not, to repeat, that defenses aren't difficulties. Both present problems in analytical treatment, but I think it is profitable to distinguish them. If we go that far, we must ask what does the patient defend?

Apparently, the patient does not defend the whole neurosis. There are certain factors he would gladly be rid of. In the first place, he would like to be rid of certain symptoms which really disturb him, like crippling anxiety, self-hate, or whatever. But it is not only the symptoms he wishes to be rid of. He wants also to be rid of his inhibitions, whatever they are. He dislikes his failure to stand up for his feelings or his beliefs, his shyness, his inability to say "no." Nevertheless, he does defend what feels to him like subjective values in the neurotic structure. Or, to put it the other way around, whenever the patient goes on the defensive, there is a subjective value involved, provided, coming back to the example of the executive of the social agency, this subjective value is not outweighed by something more important, by priorities. And these priorities, in the first place, would be his constructive forces. Still, there may also be neurotic elements among the priorities. For instance, consider the story of Ignatius Loyola: he decided at some point in his life that the career of a

saint was more important for him than his enjoying
the comforts of women. And his determination, his iron
will power to mold himself into this saintliness, was
very much more important to him than his conquest
of women. Here you have a man who decided at the
beginning of his career what he wanted. (It is difficult
to judge if, later, there were more truly religious motives
involved.) This seemed to be more important, this career
of a saint, than anything else. His determination enabled
him to renounce plenty of things which were, by contrast, not of much importance, if any at all.

In many instances, the patient's attitude towards
his own trends are divided, as we know. For instance,
many patients will cherish their vindictiveness as a
necessary weapon or as a means to vindicate themselves, to feel superior over others. But in other ways
or at other times, they will detest their vindictiveness
or be afraid of it. In an example that I cited earlier, a
patient wanted nothing more than spontaneity, but his
fear of criticism meant there was nothing more terrifying to him than spontaneity. So his attitude was
divided. There, too, we must know and not be deceived
by the patient's emphasizing his wish for something
such as independence or spontaneity. If for a long time
nothing happens on that score, if he fails to develop
what he says is his wish, we would be asking still, "What
is really at stake here? Are there certain subjective values he is defending?"

What I mean was very nicely illustrated in a novel
by Pearl Buck. A physician saw a man who had a tumor
on the back of his neck. As a physician who really cared
for the health of people, he told this man that he had

better go to a hospital to have something done about this tumor. "Oh, no," said the man, "my soul is in that tumor." So, here, he subjectively valued this tumor as his soul. Before surveying these subjective values, I want to meet one objection that easily may confuse issues. One may say here, "Is not much, if not everything in neurosis, in itself, a defense?"

If that is so, then it would mean that the defenses we see in psychoanalytic therapy are the neurotic's customary ways for defending his neurotic structure or parts of it. I think, however, this viewpoint which I have heard within our Institute—"Is not most or all of neurosis really a defense?"—is at best justified from a historico-genetic viewpoint.[3] Let's take neurotic affection or love or power. These have arisen, if you want to put it that way, as a defense against basic anxiety, as a means to feel more safe. In that way, you could call them defensive moves. If, however, you forget about the origins of such drives and look at them from the phenomenological viewpoint and just try to describe the qualities of such drives, you would say: here are drives—let's say the lust for power, drives so strong that Freud, for instance, could consider them as instinctual in nature.

But there are other neurotic positions which are more immediately defensive in their quality, which allay anxiety, and which protect against hurts or protect parts of the structure from crumbling. Take, for instance, arbitrary rightness. That's not a drive. That's primarily a defensive attitude, defensive in the sense that I am using it here: it removes self-doubts; it makes for a protective skin, like Siegfried bathing in the dragon's blood. It protects against criticism. So, the patient brings this into the analytic situation. Is that arbitrary rightness now a difficulty or a defense? I think it is both. It naturally makes for difficulty in analyzing the patient, but, again, the point that counts is whether he goes on the defensive for this rightness or examines it, regarding it as a problem to be analyzed. Now, in the course of the analysis he will do first one and then the other. But he may very well first go on the defensive and modestly say, "It so happens that I know I am right." This means that he believes himself always to be right. Or, on the other hand, he may say (as did one patient of mine) that he doesn't give a damn whether it is right or wrong, but things are just as he sees them—another way of defending this rightness. Later on, this same patient may come to regard this very rightness as a problem. He will have learned, in the meantime, what difficulty it really makes in therapy. He will have learned about himself and can accept himself better. That is, later on, he may be willing to regard this arbitrary rightness as a problem and will examine it. One could say his arbitrary rightness is at first a difficulty for which he goes on the defensive, and later, a difficulty he is willing to analyze. That is, concerning primarily defensive attitudes, we would need to speak about the defense of a defense.

Now let's make a survey of the subjective values which are defended. These subjective values are of two kinds. One consists, briefly, of *positive* values which the patient defends because he feels there is something precious involved. Then there are *protective* or *defensive* values which he doesn't cherish per se, but which he feels are indispensable as a protection against something. The equivalent would be, on a national score, that we may go on the defensive for something we regard as precious, say, our democratic way of living, and we may go on the defensive, also, for something that really serves our defense, say our military resources and military secrets. Most attitudes or defenses which we meet in analytic therapy must be regarded from both sides. Take, for instance, the drive for power in whatever form it occurs. It is something which the patient regards as a positive value. Nevertheless, it also serves as a protection against the much more dreaded feeling of helplessness.

We could also note that there are differences in the extent to which some attitudes have a defensive component—some subjective values are primarily defensive and some are primarily positive. For instance, consider the difference between a person driven towards power and the person who is likewise driven, but towards rigid self-control. The first possesses more of a positive value because he displays quite a zest for living. The second possesses what is primarily a protective value. Speaking of the positive values, what belongs among them is all that gives the person zest for living, a feeling of meaning or satisfaction, or lends a feeling of worth, strength or right.

In this category of positive values, which the patient defends, I count as the first among them the passionate drives, that which gives the neurosis a demonic character—and, after all, it was observed at one time that such persons were possessed by demons. This is a good description! People are possessed by ambition or power. Or, people are obsessed by having to reform the world, say, people like Calvin or Savonarola. Or, people are relentlessly driven towards love because they expect fulfillment and meaning to their lives.

Equally so, we include those people who are driven towards masochistic fulfillments, such as Sacher-Masoch, from whom the word masochism stems and who described it. That's where he found satisfaction. Life for him would have been pretty empty without it. You see the same driven quality in those with certain sadistic drives. I got a letter once from a person after I published *Our Inner Conflicts*. He wrote full of scorn how I was such a nincompoop. I had not the remotest idea of what a wonderful thing these sadistic drives are! They make one feel alive, he said. And they are a real drive, and so on and so forth. He said in his way that sadism made his life meaningful and that otherwise his life was pretty empty. You see the same driving force in exploiting, in bargaining, in the drive to vindictive triumph, as well as in simple, concrete vengeance. You see a similar drive, mostly more hidden, in those really driven towards the delight of tearing down and frustrating on the grounds, "I am miserable, why should others be happy?" And if one can't find enjoyment because of despair or whatever, then the only way out, the only way to get some meaning, may be to tear down, to frustrate. Here you have these drives which certainly the persons themselves will perceive as eminently positive because they make them feel alive, they give them certain thrills or satisfactions. They give meaning, a zest for living.

There are other ways that give a person a feeling

4. Difficulties and Defenses

of meaning, a very important feeling for the neurotic because he is so alienated that he must either search for it or go off living in a shallow way. This search may result in his having many friends to care for him, being acceptable to others, helping others, living through and for others as many people do in their marriages, and working—even though his working may have a compulsive character. This search, also, may be reflected in the many, many factors in neurosis that give a person a feeling of worth, of strength, or of being right. Here, I am thinking of the various kinds of prides, self-idealization itself, of the insistence of being accepted by others, on being useful to others, and so forth. Also, there are quite different ways of acquiring and maintaining a feeling of worth or a feeling of strength through a sense of mastery as, for instance, in getting back at others and gaining thereby the illusion of omnipotence. Since it is through our feelings, of course, that we feel our aliveness, our feelings of meaning and worth will be connected with positive values that are strongly defended.

I am sure this list I have made of the positive values that the patient feels are precious, is incomplete. The next list, the defensive values or protective values that the neurotic uses for keeping the positive values safe, will also be incomplete. Among these are the neurotic's own defenses against anxiety, such as distracting maneuvers, narcotizing activities like drinking, sleeping, and so forth. We could, in part at any rate, subsume under protective values the alienating defenses that reduce anxiety, the means for warding off the disruptive force of conflicts: the neurotic's denying conflicts, his compartmentalizing them, his attempts to streamline himself, his cynicism. Another kind of defense of a protective nature would be all the patient has built up against criticism, against feeling guilty, against self-contempt or self-hate. His striving to be perfect is an example of such a defense—his trying to fulfill his "shoulds," or at least holding to the illusion of fulfilling them, his rightness (thereby scratching any doubts he may have), his control, his pretenses. All of these defensive moves serve to protect against, let's say, self-contempt and self-hate, primarily, but also against criticism from the outside. Many self-effacing people avoid defeat by holding onto their restrictions, by keeping themselves down.

Returning to something more general, there are defenses against anxiety, despair, and hopelessness. These latter, despair and hopelessness—feeling the emptiness of one's life—stem ultimately from alienation, the walling off of inner experiences. One may defend against this feeling empty by distracting company, by work, by shallow living, by shallow optimism. There are all sorts of defenses against hurts and disappointments. Similarly, there are a variety of defenses against the feeling of succumbing to chaos, to feeling lost, to inertia. You see these defenses in those who need to hold onto their rigid "shoulds" because they have the feeling that there is nothing else to grip: "These 'shoulds' at least give me some rope to hang onto and bring some order into my life." Most prominent among these defenses is diffuse externalization, the tendency to experience internal processes as occurring outside oneself. One must also consider arbitrary rightness (the squelching of self-doubts). Also, consider the conviction of "getting by" as another such defense.

In analysis, all the subjective values are questioned. That may happen also outside analysis. But certainly, they are, in analysis, more systematically under attack than anywhere else in life. Hence, as long as the patient feels they are precious or indispensable, he must go on the defensive. This shows in three areas: in the work proper at his problems, in his attitude towards the therapist, and in his attitude towards therapy, as such.

The contention I have presented here is that when a patient is on the defensive, there is often a subjective value at the core of blockages and it is good to ask oneself just which subjective value is being defended. This leads in general ways to a more elaborate study of the subjective values in neurosis. Sure, we know some of these values and I have presented some here. Nevertheless, it would be very worthwhile to make a much more elaborate and definite study of these subjective values. The patient comes into analysis with his particular difficulties, much as he does when entering a job or a human relationship. These I would suggest calling the *difficulties* with which we must contend. But, to be distinguished from these difficulties are those *blockages* or *defenses* that he puts up to protect these subjective values. Success in analytic work depends upon whether he is willing to examine, to test, to delve into, to pursue a problem, and eventually to change.

5. Intellectual Process or Emotional Experience

Now we may turn to the importance of emotions in the analytic process. Briefly, there has been quite a change of attitude toward the importance of emotional experiences in analysis. When Freud made his therapeutic experiments in hypnosis—and that was quite some experimenting!—a reliving of certain past experiences was considered central. Then, as Freud went on with his research, building his theories, there was a swing more toward the intellectual side. Analysis became more a question of understanding, a question of appeal to reason. If, at that time, one would have asked, "How come the patient gets better and changes?," the answer would have been that the patient realizes that a certain attitude is really infantile (using Freud's terminology), or that a repetition of certain infantile attitudes toward experiences has been better understood. The patient's mature judgment will tell him that such attitudes are not rational, that it is no longer good to continue such attitudes. At that time, analysis made an appeal to reason. Later, that appeal, that overrating of reason and intellect started to change. I don't want to go into the whole history of these shifts. You may know the history yourself. Nevertheless, the first change came about through Ferenczi's and Rank's paper, at which time psychoanalysis was still quite grounded in the notion that infantile experiences needed to be relived.[1] But the important part of the paper was not its concentration on infantile experiences, but its emphasis on emotional experiences.

That emphasis was extended and is now very widely accepted as important and desirable. For example, Theodor Reik, who quite some years ago wrote a book on the therapeutic effect of surprise,[2] argued that if the patient is taken by surprise, he may react emotionally and that will have a therapeutic effect. Only recently, I had a talk with John Lynne in Hawaii. Last year, he gave us a quite interesting paper on the split personality.[3] Briefly, what he said was that he, too, felt the only important thing in analysis was the emotional experience. He may be going overboard in his emphasis, but he followed suggestions of other psychiatrists who had tried a certain procedure. Dr. Lynne put the patient partly under a sedative and, as I understand it, gave mild doses of electric stimulation to the thalamus. It was his impression that this combination of sedation and thalamic stimulation brought about real emotional experience.

Why I mention this at all is that here is a person

who goes his own way following the suggestion of other psychiatrists who are far removed from us. Yet he also arrives at this conclusion that emotional experiences are important for therapeutic benefit. So far, I think, there is a fairly general acceptance of the desirability of emotional experiences in psychoanalysis, in addition to merely talking about things or intellectually realizing things. However, there are many detailed questions involved, the answers to which are still fairly unclear. I will bring up just some of the problems involved.

For instance, to begin with one point, there seem to be various analysts who put particular stress on certain factors that they feel need to be experienced. For instance, I have heard Harold Kelman often stress the desirability of a patient's experiencing anxiety. Alexander Reid Martin places the emphasis on experiencing conflict.[4] He puts it in terms of the bodily participation in conflict, and I think I know what he means, though it does not have terrific meaning for me. I feel any real emotional experience has something of a totality in it. The German word *Erlebnis*, which has to do with an alive feeling, also captures this sense of totality of feeling. *Leben* has to do with aliveness, with life. It is a good word because it means something is emotionally alive and includes the totality of us. It is to be compared, for instance, with orgasm. A really good orgasm is not just a localized feeling but something that comprises all of our being. A sensation of vitality can, of course, be localized, but it would not be, then, an *Erlebnis* as I now use the term. Or, in my paper, "The Paucity of Inner Experiences," I mention the importance of experiencing emptiness, a point which Ralph Harris stressed very much at that time.[5]

All of these—anxiety, conflict, *Erlebnis,* localized vitality, inner emptiness, and so forth—are both desirable and important. But as yet I would see no particular reason to single out this-or-that factor as preeminent, though I do believe that the more something, anything, is experienced and felt—not just going on in the "brain"—the more therapeutically effective it is. Now, more specifically, what is the value of such emotional experience in the analysis?

These factors are partly self-evident. Nothing becomes as real to us as that which we directly experience. We can hear about hunger or war or the beauty of mountains or of labor pains, but they lack the same reality to us as when we, ourselves, experience pain or hunger or thirst or beauty or love, or whatever. The very same—something not being as real—applies to what goes on inside the analysis, too. I want to mention one point already alluded to several times today: one may have a perfect conviction that something is so, yet really feeling it gives it quite a different reality value. What is not felt remains, after all, an inference, an inference that may carry quite some conviction. But because it remains an inference, it does not get at big roots. It does not become the person's own property. Very often, it is difficult to distinguish real feelings from inferences because a patient may be quite productive and quite interested in something and yet, after some hours, you notice that nothing much has really taken root or really meant something to him in a deep way. It is as if he talked about possibilities, as did this patient whom I mentioned earlier in another context. We had some very good and productive hours about his fear of criticism. Though everything seemed to be clear, it was nothing but an inference he made: apparently, he must have a fear of criticism. Naturally, you also want to build upon inferences. Still, don't build altogether on them, but do so only to a greater or lesser degree.

A second value of the patient's directly experiencing something in analysis is in his feeling for the intensity of something, which, as we all know, is very important. Of course, rather than directly feel intensity one may infer intensity. If, for instance, a patient sees point for point for point the motives behind the panic she gets when something is out of control, then, by inference, control must be important. There is nothing intellectual to be said against such inferred intensity; nor does she want to dispute its value. But it is not felt. It is inferred, and it may be the inference which is held with intense conviction, not the actual feeling.

It is astounding what people do with feelings in analysis. Sometimes, patients may bring up fleeting feelings. We understand that the patient may disregard them, though to us these feelings may be important enough to pick up and see whether they are bubbles coming out of a great depth.

But even if a feeling is pretty strong, like a feeling of indignation at a frustrated claim, or an anger at something—really felt experiences—even so, patients may discard such strong feelings by saying, "Well, I have a good reason for this anger." You see, this is not true interest by the patient in his anger, but is instead interest in whether the anger is justified. What is the reason for it? Or, he might say, "I really had a terrific wave of rage—but, after all, it is not justified." Again, it is not the feeling itself that preoccupies the patient, but rather whether it is right to have the feeling. Or, he might tell of some incident where he overreacted to some insult or some occurrence, and he might say, "All right, that's an overreaction." And that's how a feeling might get put into some drawer and done away with. Or, he will ask immediately, "Why is that so? Why am I so angry?" All of this is quite different from being face to face with a feeling, *per se.*

Earlier, I gave an example of a patient's coming face to face with a strong feeling and I want to repeat it here. Although it is a simple example, we need to analyze something more about it. This episode, you may recall, occurred when the patient was on vacation from formal analysis: it was mostly a piece of self-analysis. He was on the self-effacing side, but just coming to life.

Through some provocation from the outside, you may recall, suddenly this patient felt a terrific rage for having put up with so much in his life. Incident after incident occurred to him. He didn't ask, "Was that justified? Why is that so? . . ." Nothing. No justifications. No questions or reasons: just being confronted and feeling the stark naked rage for having put up with too much all his life. Without any analysis of it, mind you, just going through the experience, he realized that his reaction could be very valuable and knew not to choke off something but just to let things come up. So he did and found it very unpleasant. But afterwards he felt an enormous liberation. He felt serene, happy.

There was none of his usual timidity toward people. He showed a friendly feeling, an openness. Now, that this result occurred without any formulated thought of analysis brings me to a third point, namely, the feeling of liberation.

I want to discuss here a few incidents concerning liberation, all of which are simple. One incident I published in one of my books and led to a very important discovery about neurotic claims.[6] To repeat it briefly: I was coming back from Mexico during World War II and, because of priorities, I was put off the plane in darkest Texas. I was at first, well, I was a little angry. But mostly I was badly fatigued and just desperate. How could I ever get to New York? I spent a pretty miserable night. But during this night on the train, gradually (I don't remember exactly how it went), instead of the fatigue, I felt rage, a rage about my situation. "That shouldn't happen to me!" Priorities are all right, but it was just a terrific—I wouldn't say insult—but it was just a terrific fate, so to speak. To be in this situation wasn't pleasant. But, lo and behold, this rage really got out in the open and I made the intellectual connection that there must be a claim. Actually, the claim was not directly felt. Still, it was the only thing I could come up with—and it was absolutely right—here was a claim I had for something extra special. At that moment, I had an enormous feeling of liberation. Rarely in my life have I been so happy. Despite my riding in a coach three days and four nights, and certainly the ride was just as unpleasant as before my insight, I felt very happy. I felt serene. I enjoyed looking out the window. I enjoyed talking with the other people. It was really a wonderful experience. I bring it up here because it lends special emphasis to the feeling of liberation which I wish to explore further.

Specifically, I wish to explore the therapeutic value contained in the feeling of liberation. In the experience I just described, my having to go by train caused me to have an emotional upheaval of rage and vindictiveness—maybe that the plane I had been put off would crash. This, and my claim, my insisting on something extra special, struck a chord. What happened was not the deliberate and conscious relinquishing of this claim. Apparently, it just fell away. The dropping out of an insistence on something extra or the claim for exemption, however you would call it, was certainly a relief. That we can understand. So besides being an emotional experience, it was in addition a piece of good analysis in that feelings of rage and vindictiveness were connected with the claim underlying it. You could also interpret this experience as a surrender, of my having relinquished or surrendered certain neurotic factors and therefore feeling more at one with myself. Still again, instead of speaking of claims, you could say that something, some egocentricity, was at least temporarily done away with.

I wonder, though, if that is really what this experience of liberation is about. If you think about the experience of the patient who raged about tolerating too much from people, there was no analysis whatever. There was just this stark naked feeling of rage for having put up with too much. We must think here of one general factor, namely, getting in touch with something very vital. After all, rage is vital. This may be particularly important for people who are on the self-effacing side and, therefore, have a restriction particularly on anything which is wild and untamed. But it is also true that such restriction applies to many neuroses and is equally present for the resigned type and for many arrogant vindictive types with their checks on feelings. After all, in every neurosis there is a check on vitality. The mere getting in touch with something vital in oneself, I believe, does have a liberating effect. While considering this, I thought again of the description which William Henry Hudson gave of certain landscapes and how profoundly he was affected by the Patagonian landscape. He felt happy and liberated. The landscape brought him into contact with something vital, powerful, and untamed within himself.

Consider a patient of mine who frequently complained about emotional deadness. Recently, when he came up with certain rages that followed his not having his own way, I said, "It would be very good if you really would experience these rages more. No matter what they are or from what source they arise, they are, after all, something very vital—what you feel!"

To be more specific, I wish I return to the patient with self-effacing trends who had put up with too much from others, from himself, and had not dared to fight and encounter all that goes into facing this in himself. There is something in his insight that connotes a breaking of chains. Here, for the first time, is emotional rebellion—somebody who breaks his handcuffs, breaks chains, and says to himself, "That need not continue all my life!" We could see this hopeful feeling as arising with a rebellion against feeling subdued all his life. In this case, we see another instance of the feeling of liberation as having therapeutic benefit.

Also, quite different factors enter into some other experiences. I mentioned one of them in the paper "The Paucity of Inner Experiences." The experience of emptiness which is frightening in itself may often, if it occurs at the proper time, arouse very constructive and alive feelings. What we must think is: "Is this a real experience of the meaninglessness of one's life, or is it the feeling of emptiness?" This terrifying feeling of not living can arouse some countermoves by constructive forces. This mobilization of countermoves by constructive forces in a person offers a very different explanation for how feeling impoverished can produce therapeutic benefit. This explanation may also apply to the feeling of liberation.

However, I think there is one more factor we must think of when considering the reason for the therapeutic effect of intense feeling. This last factor, which I want to discuss here, has something to do with self-acceptance. Though this became pretty self-evident to me after I had thought it through, it was not at all so at first. I just want to present, here, the road along which I arrived at this result.

I asked myself, "There are, after all, during the analytic process, many patients who feel strong emotions. They may feel anger, rage, abused, despair, hopelessness, self-contempt, self-reproach. And these feelings, even though they are really felt, often have no therapeutic effect. Why?" So, apparently we have to qualify: what are the conditions under which they are just strong emotions with no therapeutic effect?

One patient, if you turn again to the example of this man who put up with too much in his life, did have an experience of feeling abused and he raged about it. He gained something through these strong emotions. Another patient, as you all have seen, may express vividly feelings of being abused, yet those feelings have no therapeutic effect whatsoever. What is the difference?

The patient who feels abused and then feels rage and indignation and who very freely expresses these feelings indicates a neurotic feeling, to put it bluntly. But so did the patient who felt rage about putting up with too much. There must be some difference in the value of such intense feelings, a value determined by whether or not such feelings were hitherto suppressed. In the case of the patient who had this wholesome rage, his rage had been suppressed. That is to say, he had long-standing divided feelings about the rage and yet, now, he apparently could afford to experience the rage despite whatever there was in him that was against it. It was in this spirit: "I want to experience whatever is there." In my own experience with the airlines, there was no such determination. For me, it was probably the stress of feeling miserable in that whole situation which brought about such an emotional commotion. I now believe that such a wholesome experience can be therapeutically valuable only if it is without condemnation, without justification, without embellishment, and without any interest in the reasons for the feeling—just the experience of the emotion itself. In this, my own experience is similar to the case of the man who put up with too much. For both of us the question was "What do I feel?"—nothing at all like "Have I a right?" or "How do I feel it?" or whatever.

All of this—experiences of liberation and of intense emotion—points to an aspect of therapeutic effect. Such experiences give the patient a stronger feeling of "I"— it is actually the expression of accepting oneself as one is and not just with one's intellect, but of accepting oneself feelingly at the time: "This is me!" This is unaccompanied by fringe intellectualizations or judgments. I think this is a point about which we could have some discussion, that the feeling of liberation which occurs quite often after such strong experiences has something to do with a feeling of peace, a feeling of self-acceptance on a very deep emotional level, of being at one with oneself. It is really an experience of what we call the "real self." The best example of "real self" experiences, I think, is the one of this man with the pure rage without any intellectual connections. It means accepting himself as he is. Put in theoretical terms, it means accepting his "actual self." Nothing has changed, as yet. Sure, later on he might be more interested in understanding this rage and do something about it. But, at the moment, there is nothing changed—just the experience of such acceptance. This has very far-reaching therapeutic implications. If this self-feeling, this self-acceptance, is so important, then maybe we have to change a lot about our therapy.

Of course, I also feel it is important to avoid going overboard with the value of emotional experience, as if such experience is all there is to analysis. I don't think that is right. Years ago, I think after a lecture of Alexander Reid Martin, somebody said that the pur-

pose of analysis was to convey emotional experiences.
I had misgivings about that. There is plenty of other
work to be done, such as seeing connections and realizing something intellectually—anything that has to do
with the whole of us. But I believe that nothing works
as effectively as experience. Consider the two emotional experiences that I tried to analyze. I had to do
quite some work after my airline experience and with
whatever other claims were there. The liberation was,
after all, a temporary experience, though so profound
that I never could forget it. It aroused plenty of stimulation and created plenty more work to be done. This
same liberation that I mentioned earlier in the case of
the man who had stark naked rage, was likewise stim-
ulating and transitory. There was quite a period in which
he did not get on with anything in spite of his wanting
to, because he had to find access to certain expansive
trends of his. So, the direct and immediate experience
of feelings is certainly no panacea and we shouldn't go
overboard with it. Still, I think it is very important.

Nevertheless, there is the question, how can we help
the patient to experience more in the analysis? There
are the various ways that I have mentioned already.
But now I will discuss three factors that address this
question.

One factor concerns the analyst's becoming more
and more sensitive to what is really felt, as opposed to
what is talk or inference. That, I feel, is the basis on
which we can become effective in time. Now, sometimes the distinction between what is felt and what is
only talk is fairly obvious to you. The patient whom
you help to become more sensitive will become, him-

self, more aware of when he is just talking about something and not really in the situation, or when he is really interested and feeling something. You may sometimes, if you have doubts on this score, ask the patient a direct question. And here is one little piece of training for yourself that I would suggest: every now and then, review just for yourself a piece of analysis. To get a good perspective on it, the piece you select may need to be from some time before. Or, perhaps you might choose from some of your personal analytical experiences. Again, this may prove most useful after some time has passed. Try to make a clear analysis of what was really felt, what was only vaguely felt, and what was inference, and right and good inference. Reviews of this kind may be a help in becoming more sensitive to these differences, in time.

I have an example of a simple incident, which I have published, and which further illuminates the value of reexamining a piece of analysis.[7] A woman suddenly became afraid of a dog when she wanted to take a walk to a mountain top. She performed a very good piece of analysis, arriving at the result that her fear was due to self-contempt and that this self-contempt arose because she felt she should be able to make the walk up. After the self-analysis, her fear disappeared. But something remained in her of the connection between being afraid and feeling ashamed, humiliated, and so forth.

Now we may analyze that simple episode further. An incidental finding is its showing that we can have some quite good results with comparatively little being said. We can recognize that the fear of the dog was certainly felt. The self-contempt, however, was felt vaguely. She felt cowardly; she felt clumsy; she felt awkward; she felt that other people might look down on her for being overcautious. That is, I do not believe she had a full experience of self-contempt, but instead something coming close to it. The self-contempt was quite unjustified in this situation and had to do with certain demands she placed on herself: she should be able to climb the mountain, no matter how she was dressed, how the weather was, how her shoes were, whether she had a walking stick or not. She should be able to walk up. That part, her self-contempt for failing her own standards, was pure inference. So, while this piece of analysis helped at that time, if I would have insisted more upon clarifying the emotional components, the effect of this analysis might have been more lasting.

A second way in which we can help the patient experience more in the analysis is to analyze all the factors which prevent a person from experiencing his insights. Now, there are many factors, and I have discussed some of them in the paper "The Paucity of Inner Experiences." Briefly, I believe that those factors which connote that a patient wants to be something or feels he should be something different from what he really is, make for a lack of interest in his real being. To undertake the analysis of all these factors is quite a big overall order, so to speak. It means analyzing the "shoulds," but doing so from the viewpoint of how little that person accepts himself. Recently, for example, I said something about self-acceptance to a patient in analysis, a man who felt not only indignant about most people but who also felt very inferior about himself. He said, "Oh, no. You are all wrong. That is the one thing I do! I am altogether self-accepting." As it turned out, he had fixed it in his mind that self-acceptance is a good thing, which is true. He had a real conviction about that. But he forgot or lacked interest in whether he really did accept himself, that is to say, his real being. This occurs so very often. You need not even go so far as to the idealized image. People fix in their minds their independence because independence is a good thing, or accepting criticism because being able to accept constructive criticism is a good thing—so they get positively uninterested in how they really are. Now, those are just a few examples of how fixed ideas can prevent experiencing more in analysis, but you know yourself that analyzing this comprises consideration of many factors. I think, however, that whatever one analyzes, one should draw the connection for the patient, at least in one's own mind, to what it means in terms of self-acceptance.

The third kind of help would be direct encouragement. That can be done in various ways. One is to encourage the expression or the taking seriously of fleeting and abortive feelings. Just a little example from recent days: a patient talked about something which seemed to me very pertinent, but she said, "I have the feeling that this doesn't really interest me because I feel worried about something." She didn't know what it was. So, I did not only say (what we all would), "Let's go, by all means, to what you are worried about," but I explicitly said it was so good that she really felt this, that she was worried about something. She was aware of a feeling and could express it seriously. Or, similarly, if you approach the patient with some comment or observation, he may express, "I feel a vague uneasiness—as if I want to get away from what you are saying." That means it is good not only to go after his wish to run away, but to explicitly encourage such awareness of feeling.

We can take an approach still more radical than only encouraging awareness of feeling. We can go beyond saying, "It would be good if you felt that more," or asking a question about such feeling. As I encourage general awareness of feeling more and more, I find myself encouraging a patient to live with a specific feeling. Take as an example the fear of criticism that arises in a person who has it fixed in his mind that he is very independent. He doesn't like to recognize in himself the fear of criticism and stay with it. Such encouragement to stay with a specific feeling is good therapy. If he wants to go into reasons and to understand his fear of criticism, say, the analyst could tell him first that the most important thing is the true experience of this fear of criticism in his daily living, that he live with it, and that we'll find out in time what it means. Another example I mentioned earlier concerned the patient who saw that certain rages of his had to do with his not having his own way. Again, I told him it would be good if he could live with that, if he could feel his rages whenever they come up.

Now this is a critical question, of course: Can the patient do it? Is the patient far enough along to accept himself? I think the crucial factor, really, is to experience without embellishment and condemnation. By the way, in a session today I said something that illustrates analyzing or making aware for the patient those factors interfering with insight or feeling. I said to a patient that it would be good if she became aware of her constant moralizing tendency, that she really could not feel anything without putting a judgment on it—good, bad, moral, immoral, and so on. To be aware of feelings, to live with them, to experience what she really felt would help so much. This occurred to me because if we put this emphasis on feeling and live with something and experience it, we are freed from any judgmental inclinations we may have more than anything I know. Even if we don't feel any judgmental attitude, the simple fact of analyzing the bad consequences of some attitude, like the fear of criticism, what it does to a person, or whatever, will lead a patient to immediately feel, "So this fear of criticism is not good." Although we do not condemn the feeling, he will believe that we do. Now, without knowing it, many analysts still are moralizing much too much. That is to say, there is too automatic a judgment of something being good or bad. This approach with oneself or to others, to experience and feel, does away with any such judgments in a most radical way.

Karen Horney died December 4, 1952.

105

Karen Horney,
A Reminiscence

by
EDWARD R. CLEMMENS

This small collection of Horney's lectures on psychoanalytic technique is a tribute to the memory of the
founder of the Association for the Advancement of
Psychoanalysis and the American Institute for Psychoanalysis.[1] Thirty-four years have passed since she stood
in front of us and delivered her ideas in her inimitable
way, unconcerned about syntax and purity of diction,
but enormously concerned with what she had to say
and how to involve her listeners. I was one of them, a
junior candidate in training at the time, auditing a
course open for academic credit only to senior candidates. None of us knew, or even suspected, that these
five lectures were to be Horney's last ones. The other
fifteen, which she had planned to deliver, are known
only by their titles which were published in the Institute curriculum, their content vaguely remembered by
those of her students who had listened to a similar

course two years earlier. However, no recording was taken at that time. The present five lectures were preserved on tape and this is what makes them unique.

I was unaware of their existence, until they were made available to me this past summer. Listening to Karen Horney's voice was for me a moving experience.

There was about her an air of wholeness, of certainty, of total dedication and commitment, of a conviction that her ideas were valuable, that they were worth sharing with colleagues and students, because knowing them would make a difference to helping those in need.

Several years before I heard Karen Horney speak for the first time, I had read some of her books. I had felt then, what so many of her readers have described— i.e., that she was addressing me, that her grasp of human nature was more intimate than that of other authors, that she was not a detached clinical observer, but a concerned friend who was eager to help.

When I first heard her speak, this earlier impression was strengthened, but also changed somewhat. Her writing, after all, was carefully edited. Whatever idiosyncratic material might have existed in an early draft, had probably been erased or muted. The looseness and aliveness of her speech—its absence of formality, its easy humor—came as a surprise to me.

Printed words acquire an air of finality. Karen Horney's spontaneity in the flesh was thus somewhat of a shock to me.

During the long years since she left us, I have never lost contact with her thoughts. Her ideas, more than anyone else's, have guided me in my work as an analyst. Her students, who became my teachers, conveyed her thoughts to me in a multitude of ways, filtered through each one's understanding of her. Different interpretations have led to a variety of views, even opposing ones, that reflect the predilections of their presenters. Such is the fate of many original works. Commentaries are written when the founder's opinion can no longer be ascertained. Early commentaries are followed by commentaries on commentaries. What once was live thought becomes fossilized. Minute dissection leads to the establishment of doctrinal teaching, a sad fate indeed.

How fortunate then, that Horney's spoken word can still reach us. Even with some technical imperfections it is a treasure trove of fresh, spontaneous expression. The text, as published in this small volume, is as close to a faithful transcript, as was possible. Douglas H. Ingram's editing was done with the utmost care and respect to the original. Unnecessary repetitions and redundancies were omitted, some obscure syntax straightened out, not much more. Nonetheless, reading the printed page conveys a different image than does listening to the tapes. The tapes are closer to reality, a reality that may be less perfect, less smooth and more searching, but also more authentic. Horney's tone of voice, her slightly ironic mannerisms, are unavoidably lost in print. Had today's technology existed then, we might be able to watch her and listen to her on video. However, no record can duplicate life fully. Something is always lost.

At the risk of provoking controversy I shall describe

this elusive "something" as I perceived it. I will not attempt to objectify my subjective impressions, not only because they won't be shared by other colleagues who knew her, but because I believe that my subjective impressions are just that, emotionally charged reminiscences that are mine alone. The diversity of memories may enrich all of us, as long as we can manage to tolerate differences and disagreements.

To me Karen Horney's style was intensely familiar. I only heard her speak in English, but with a heavy German accent. The way she pronounced some words resembled the diction that I was trying to banish from my own speech. However, this familiarity went beyond accents. Her mannerisms were German, the way she let her voice trail off with a quick succession of "and so on, and so forth," the slight gesture or a nod that invited agreement from the audience (and usually obtained it), even when some listeners had not fully understood what they were agreeing with. This central European flavor had nothing to do with the ill-bred pomposity of the Nazi style. To the contrary, it was the elegant light touch of cosmopolitan pre-war Europe at its best, it was Berlin in the 1920s. It was cultured without pretentiousness, knowledgeable and witty, and it also was unself-conscious, without the painful scars that are the curse of oppressed minorities. She seemed comfortable with the way she was, an individualist through and through, not much interested in movements and isms.

I remember an occasion, when she spoke a few days after having heard J. Edgar Hoover address an American Psychiatric Association convention to remind the psychiatric establishment of their civic duty. He had told his audience that psychiatrists were in the unique position of being told by some of their patients about their subversive activities. In view of what he regarded as the grave danger of the communist conspiracy, Hoover felt that it was the patriotic duty of psychiatrists to inform the FBI of any such revelations.

Horney did not use the occasion to give an impassioned speech. She simply stated that this was a decision that everyone had to make for himself and that she would rather go to jail than betray a patient's confidence. She might have commented on the stupidity of assuming that conspirators, revolutionaries and spies were likely to be found on analysts' couches. She might have said something about the evil of the Nazi police state, the preciousness of freedom and her own democratic convictions. However, she did not touch upon these points at all. It simply was not her style, she stayed clear of politics.

I sensed that she was too skeptical to believe that some kind of millennium would result from the victory of any political movement. She had seen several of them and was the wiser for the experience. Not that she had become jaded! To the contrary, she had preserved her youthful vitality, curiosity, and zest for living. She had never become a cynic.

There was a wholesomeness about her, a capacity for joy and enthusiasm that was contagious. I believe that these qualities, more than the intellectual underpinnings of her theories, accounted for her success as an analyst and a teacher, as well as her appeal to the lay public. It was her personal magnetism, a rare gift among analysts and maybe among all serious and dedicated scientists.

She must have been aware of all this, I cannot believe otherwise. These traits certainly colored her relations with her followers at the Institute. There was no doubt that she occupied center stage. The Institute would have been unthinkable without her. A number of competent and dedicated colleagues made up the faculty. Some of them made remarkable contributions of their own. The success of their labors, however, was measured in terms of the acceptance of their ideas by Karen Horney. She was the final arbiter. Her opinions were listened to with deference and respect, they were not challenged, only questioned in the most measured and careful of ways.

I remember asking myself how Horney could tolerate being placed in such an exalted position. One answer was that she was indeed head and shoulders above her followers in competence, creativity, and wisdom. There were others who were her equals, and maybe even betters, in intellectual endowment alone, colleagues who were capable of eloquence, whose rhetorical skills clearly surpassed hers. Some were better at deductive reasoning, at which she did not excel. However, none possessed the combination of her talents.

She would listen to their discussions attentively, yet was ready to dismiss those points that she did not agree with lightly, even by stating that she was not much interested in the argument.

Nonetheless, a certain uneasiness on her part manifested itself in a variety of ways, several of which are quite apparent in these lectures. In her first lecture she flattered her audience by proposing to make the course a "research project." However, she never explained what she meant by this remark, nor did she subsequently return to it. I felt at the time, and even more now, that she could not have seriously believed that the format of this teaching course could have been magically transformed into a piece of research. Nor were the comments by most of the candidates of a sufficient caliber to allow for such a transformation. At best, I suppose, it was Horney's intent to elicit enthusiasm on the part of the candidates, to encourage their constructiveness, even by using an exaggerated concept.

It must strike anyone who knew Horney as odd that she concluded her first lecture by dismissing the distinction between gifted therapists and less gifted ones, emphasizing instead the importance of training. This, I believe, is a spurious argument. The two issues, as she presented them, do not belong on the same plane. They are not relevant to each other. Few of us will deny that people vary enormously in their gifts, be they intelligence, perceptivity, sensitivity, or anything else. All of us will profit by training, by learning, by sharpening our skills. Differences, however, will remain and it seems senseless to deny them.

I suspect that Horney's motive in emphasizing training over innate ability was political. She had founded a training institute and felt it necessary to convince her students of the importance of training. Training is a variable, whereas giftedness is not. By stressing the importance of training she may have

wished to encourage all of her students. Stressing giftedness may flatter some and discourage many. However, by de-emphasizing the importance of gifts, she
de-emphasized her own giftedness.

On another occasion I heard her discuss whether
certain analysts are better fitted to treat certain patients,
whether there is such a "fit," including the gender of
both patient and analyst. Horney tended to downplay
the entire issue, stressing competence and wholeheartedness instead. She recommended that a new
patient's dislike for an analyst, or a woman's objection
to a male analyst's gender, be analyzed rather than
deferred to. I still find this opinion unnecessarily arbitrary, since both approaches have merit, are not contradictory, and are certainly not mutually exclusive.

Horney's strength was most impressive in her intuitive grasp of meaning and connections in human
emotions. She struggled valiantly to build a cohesive
theory to give structure to her findings. As her understanding grew, she kept revising her theories and never
claimed to have completed her work. She admitted that
defining logical structures was difficult for her, whereas
the intuitive grasp of human emotions and their
meaning came easily and naturally. That she nonetheless succeeded in devising a conceptual framework that
hangs together makes her accomplishment even more
admirable.

It also serves as a reminder that metapsychology is
not an end in itself, that it is inadvisable to put too
much faith in principles, as though principles were more
certain than observations. Horney herself in these lectures uses her own concepts and terminology most

sparingly. By contrast, her followers then and now, tend to overuse them, as though they were givens.

She was a free spirit, intensely in touch with herself, an enormously talented analyst, a courageous innovator, a fascinating teacher who was listened to in spite of her modest oratorical skills. She denied—unsuccessfully, I think—the importance of inborn gifts. The enormous impact that she had on those who came near her, is the most convincing refutation of her own argument.

NOTES

Introduction

1. *[Page 11]* The list of lectures she intended, as provided by the Institute catalogue, suggests just how she defined her topic. The lectures are listed as follows:

   1. Free associations and the use of the couch
   2. The quality of the analyst's attention
   3. Specific psychoanalytic means of understanding the patient
   4. Interpretations: meaning and aims
   5. Timing of interpretations
   6. Consistency of interpretations
   7. Form and spirit of interpretations
   8. The patient's reactions to interpretations: validity
   9. Intellectual process or emotional experience
   10. Retarding forces: blockages
   11. Dealing with blockages
   12, 13. Mobilizing forces toward self realization
   14. The patient's attitude toward the analyst
   15, 16. The personal equation of the analyst

17. Dealing with conflicts
18. Dealing with central inner conflicts
19. Critical situations: giving advice
20. Evaluating the patient's progress: termination

In this volume the lecture entitled "Difficulties and Defenses" may correspond with catalogue entry 10, "Retarding forces: blockages."

1. THE QUALITY OF THE ANALYST'S ATTENTION

1. *[Page 15]* Perhaps restricting the course to senior candidates was Horney's intention. In fact, many others attended, including Dr. Clemmens who, in his reminiscence, notes that he was then a junior candidate.

2. *[Page 18]* The quality of the therapist's attention has been a crucial matter since Freud's 1912 paper, "Recommendations for Physicians on the Psycho-Analytic Method of Treatment." He advises psychoanalysts to maintain an "evenly hovering attention. ... All conscious exertion is to be withheld from the capacity for attention, and one's 'unconscious memory' is to be given full play; or to express it in terms of technique, pure and simple: One has simply to listen and not to trouble to keep in mind anything in particular." (*Collected Papers of Sigmund Freud*, authorized trans. under the supervision of Joan Riviere [New York: Basic Books, 1959], 2: 323–34.)

Although Horney's emphasis follows Freud's, it is more inclusive. Horney's interest in Zen and oriental philosophies finds particular application in the question of the analyst's attention. In much the same way that she found contemporary American culture to warrant a view of human psychology different from that propounded by Freud, she finds Eastern culture to offer something useful in connection with technical considerations.

3. *[Page 23]* The reader familiar with Horney's work will readily appreciate references to her theory of neurosis. Those unfamiliar with Horney's orientation are recommended to her

books in which she details her theory, especially *Neurosis and Human Growth* (New York: W. W. Norton & Co., 1950) and *Our Inner Conflicts* (New York: W. W. Norton and Co., 1945).

4. *[Page 24]* Harold Kelman, M.D., was a distinguished psychoanalyst and teacher of Horney's theory. His views are elaborated in *Helping People* (New York: Science House, 1971).

5. *[Page 25]* The series of lectures that comprise the current volume does not include observations on the analyst's personal equation. From prior courses on analytic technique, the *American Journal of Psychoanalysis,* published by the Association for the Advancement of Psychoanalysis, compiled from student notes Horney's views on technical matters. "The Analyst's Personal Equation" by Louis Azorin may be found in the *Journal,* 17: 34–8 (1957).

6. *[Page 27]* William Henry Hudson (1841–1922) was a British naturalist and writer born in Argentina of American parents. His many books display a deep sensitivity to human as well as wild life.

7. *[Page 30]* Horney's comments on note-taking are concordant with those of Freud. The analyst's receptivity and integration of what happens in the therapy session can be recorded for subsequent review, but note-taking is a very minor tool. Still, it happens that in the course of analytic training, conscientious attention to the work of learning analysis may lead the trainee to depend excessively on notes. It is conscientiousness, technical skill, and intuitive understanding, not note-taking, that are fundamental. The tendency to produce both copious notes and good results in therapy may proceed, each separately, from these fundamentals.

Though one might suppose that audio and video recordings eliminate the whole issue of note-taking, there has been considerable resistance within the analytic community to new technology. Justification for this reluctance lies in the appreciation that any recording device alters the direct, immediate, and the transient nature of communication. The person of the analyst, his understanding and empathy, is the sole instrument of the therapeutic endeavor. Nevertheless, audio and video recording are of proven value in the hands of certain teachers and therapists. (See, for example, Ian Alger's article, "Audio Visual Techniques in Psychotherapy," in the *International Encyclopedia of Psychiatry, Psychology, Psychoanalysis, and Neurology* [New York: Aesculapius, 1977.])

8. *[Page 30]* Harold G. Wolff worked at the Cornell Medical Center in the 1930s and 1940s. His studies on the effect of emotion on the flow of gastric acid contributed much to the comprehension of the physiology of emotion.

9. *[Page 31]* Validation of the therapeutic effectiveness is a continuing concern in psychotherapy and has been approached by numerous workers. Horney does not provide the categories of checks for determining the accuracy of the analyst's interventions. If we speculate that therapy is a transactive process, as John Spiegel has emphasized in *Transactions* (New York: Jason Aronson, 1971), the sense of what is said and done is a function of the therapeutic system experienced as a whole. How the quality of this system is rated, the *feel* of the work in therapy, is a major determinant of how accurate the therapist's efforts are. The patient needs to experience the therapist as understanding though perhaps not overtly sympathetic with everything the patient has to say.

A second major check for the accuracy of the analyst's interventions is the occurence and acceptance in the patient of insights. These are integrated and result in a broader range of what the patient can introduce into therapy sessions. The patient's inner world of self- and object-representations, his cognitive and affective range, is extended. The new material that spontaneously results in the form of fantasies, dreams, memories, nuance of feeling, and acknowledgment of attitudes towards the therapist, illuminates further the nature of the patient's unconscious process. It produces growing feelings of authenticity, centeredness, and relief from overt symptoms.

A third check is experience in the analyst of insights concerning the patient, the course of therapy, and even himself. That is, as the cognitive and affective range for the patient is enhanced, so it is also extended for the analyst in connection with the patient.

The fourth check on the accuracy of the analyst's interventions is the progress of the patient during therapy in more conventional terms. Although we seek evidence of an enlarging inner world for the patient, we need to recognize some correlation between this inner growth and the patient's relation to the outer world, primarily in occupational, social, and recreational spheres.

10. *[Page 32]* Presented years before the works of Michael Polanyi and Thomas Kuhn who both contributed so much to our reappraisal of the nature of how sciences change, Horney's discussion of this topic is thin by contemporary standards. For a rich account of the question of psychoanalysis-as-science, see Arnold Modell's essay, "The Nature of Psychoanalytic Knowledge," in his volume *Psychoanalysis in a New Context* (New York: Int. U. Press, 1984). See also, Dr. Clemmens's remarks in this volume.

2. FREE ASSOCIATIONS AND THE USE OF THE COUCH

1. *[Page 33]* The passage is from Eckermann's observations while he was accompanying young Goethe on the latter's Italian journey. It originally appeared in English in *Conversations of Goethe with Eckermann and Soret,* translated from the German by John Oxenford, [London: George Bell and Sons, 1874].

2. *[Page 36]* Erich Fromm, "Die Gesellschaftliche Bedingtheit der Psychoanalytischen Therapie," *Zeitschrift fr Sozialforschung,* vol. 4, *[Heft 3],* (1935):365–97.

3. *[Page 36]* Whatever witticisms Horney had in mind concerning free associations are lost. She was probably alluding to the paradox inherent in what is known as the "basic rule." The basic rule for the patient in psychoanalysis is the obligation to speak freely whatever comes to mind, to free associate. When speaking with absolute freedom is a rule, what then is the nature of freedom?

4. *[Page 48]* Lucidity, concreteness, and pertinence of free asso-

ciations are rare indeed. When effort and preparation are present in what is said then spontaneity is diminished, perhaps severely so if the patient is truly circumstantial. When spontaneous effort-free associations are present, integrity of the highest order is requisite if what the patient reports about events is to be lucid and accurate.

3. SPECIFIC PSYCHOANALYTIC MEANS OF UNDERSTANDING THE PATIENT

1. *[Page 53]* There is no available published reference in which Horney develops her concept of repetitive patterns of associations. Nevertheless, in the next paragraph of text, Horney provides an excellent example of just such a repetitive sequence.

2. *[Page 65]* Horney's concept of the idealized image shows some similarities with the grandiose self as elaborated by Heinz Kohut in *The Restoration of the Self* (New York: Int. U. Press, 1977). For a considered comparison of alternate conceptions of narcissism, see *The American Journal of Psychoanalysis,* 41 (1981):289–355.

3. *[Page 66]* From the *Plays of Ibsen,* vol. 3, trans. Michael Meyer (New York: Washington Square Press, 1986).

4. DIFFICULTIES AND DEFENSES

1. *[Page 71]* Freida Fromm-Reichmann, M.D., was among the foremost psychotherapists of Horney's era, working predominantly with psychotic patients at Chestnut Lodge in Maryland. She conjoined the perspectives of Freud and Harry Stack Sullivan. See her *Principles of Intensive Psychotherapy* (U. of Chicago Press, 1950).

2. *[Page 72]* Although Horney valued the fundamental contributions of Freud to the topography of the unconscious and to the conduct of psychoanalytic technique, she challenged his conclusions to the extent that his theory was biological and instinctivistic. In particular, she rejected Freud's insistence on penis envy as the primary determinant of feminine psychology, his instinctivistic orientation, including the libido and death

instincts, and the unresolved oedipal conflict as the pre-eminent source of psychopathology. In her view, this instinctivistic orientation was unwarranted and misleading.

Similarly, repetition compulsion, a fundamental Freudian concept that holds infantile trauma to be repeatedly experienced in disguised forms throughout life, struck Horney as lacking appreciation for the crucial fact that personalities do evolve and change. For Horney, it seemed more useful to regard neurosis as a continuing process, a deviant path requiring more and more self-deception and unconscious defensiveness.

Horney differed from Freud, too, in her insistence that science, including psychoanalysis, contains ethical positions. The psychoanalyst needs to appreciate his own beliefs and morals, distinguishing them from those of his patients. For Horney, we are all children of our culture. Freud strived vainly to ensure that the practice of psychoanalysis would not be tainted by moral conception. Contemporary philosophy has increasingly vindicated Horney's view that values ramify even pure science.

Finally, Freud and Horney differed in their vision of humankind. Whereas Freud held that the person, at best, can channel (or sublimate) instincts, Horney held that the person can adaptively liberate his constructiveness, appreciate his limitations within the structuring frame of culture, and fully participate in the process of self-realization.

For a critical appraisal of Horney's theory, as set forth in her volume *New Ways in Psychoanalysis* (New York: W. W. Norton and Co., 1939), by an eminent if somewhat maverick psychoanalyst from within the classical Freudian camp, see *The Scope of Psychoanalysis: Selected Papers of Franz Alexander, 1921–61* (New York: Basic Books, 1961). According to Jack L. Rubins in *Karen Horney: Gentle Rebel of Psychoanalysis* (New York: Dial, 1978, p. 186), Alexander later acknowledged his failure to appreciate Horney's views.

3. *[Page 81]* One of the thrusts of this lecture is that the classical analytic conception of resistance is less useful than a clear attention to whether the patient develops a defensive posture at certain times in the course of analytic sessions. She uses the

term *obstructive forces* to refer to how the neurotic blockages show, generally, including how they show within the analytic session. In other words, the concept of obstructive forces seems to more clearly correlate with Freud's concept of resistance. She is asking us to consider the value of what in ordinary compmon parlance is simply called defensiveness.

5. INTELLECTUAL PROCESS OR EMOTIONAL EXPERIENCE

1. *[Page 89]* See Sandor Ferenczi and Otto Rank's volume, *The Development of Psychoanalysis* (New York: Nerv. and Ment. Dis. Pub. Co., 1925).

2. *[Page 89]* Theodor Reik, *Surprise and the Psychoanalyst* (New York: E. P. Dutton and Co., 1937).

3. *[Page 89]* This paper, "Dynamics of Multiple Personality," by John G. Lynne, is summarized in *The American Journal of Psychoanalysis*, 12 (1952):95–96.

4. *[Page 90]* Alexander Reid Martin, M.D., was a prominent teacher and training psychoanalyst at the American Institute for Psychoanalysis. See "Tribute to Alexander Reid Martin" in *The American Journal of Psychoanalysis*, 46 (1986):91–121.

5. *[Page 91]* Ralph Harris, M.D., was a student and colleague of Karen Horney. The paper to which she refers, "The Paucity of Inner Experiences" appears in *The American Journal of Psychoanalysis*, 12 (1952):3–9.

6. *[Page 94]* In *Neurosis and Human Growth*, 44.

7. *[Page 101]* Ibid., 101–102.

KAREN HORNEY, A REMINISCENCE

1. *[Page 107]* With colleagues, Karen Horney founded the Association for the Advancement of Psychoanalysis and the American Institute for Psychoanalysis in 1941. Both organizations, as well as the Karen Horney Clinic, founded after Horney's death, are in New York City.

INDEX